THE ECONOMIC
PRESCRIPTION
FOR DEVELOPING
COUNTRIES

BY

Mahfoud B. Sellama

MASTER'S IN INTERNATIONAL RELATIONS AND
CONFLICT RESOLUTION

Graduate From American Public University

West Virginia, USA

ISBN:

Hardcover: 978-1-966565-85-7
Paperback: 978-1-966565-86-4

Editorial Review – The Economic Prescription for Developing Countries

Dear Mr. Sellama,

We hope this letter finds you well. We are glad to work on your draft and we must admit that it is quite unique in nature and it offers a wide range of solutions to the problems that are still prevalent in developing countries. In our professional opinion, we are comfortable to say that it addresses an exclusive theme and it is indeed a very well-researched peace. It is our great pleasure to proofread it, and for us, it certainly is a learning process. The information is compelling and well-developed to easily move the audience. No aspect of the draft is a drag; every other topic is as interesting as the previous one and contributes a new piece of information, eventually adding up to an elaborative book.

Now, we will look into every aspect in detail.

Tonality

The tone of *The Economic Prescription for Developing Countries* is both practical and easy to understand. The book talks about the big problems like poverty, political instability, and fixing the economy in simple language so that the readers can easily follow along. The writer's voice is strong and focused on giving real solutions while also making readers feel hopeful and ready to act. The book makes readers think about their own countries and how big changes could make things better. It explains problems like corruption, relying too much on richer countries, and government delays in a way that feels real and relatable, especially for people in developing countries. The tone is friendly and caring, making it easy for readers from all kinds of backgrounds to connect with the ideas. At the same time, it pushes readers to take action and think about new ways to solve problems.

Plot

The main idea of the book is to look at why some countries stay underdeveloped and show how they can improve their economy and government. The author talks about important problems like need deprivations, unstable governments, and corruption while also pointing out what systems and rules need to be fixed. Sellama explains how countries can use their resources, such as land, workers, money, and business ideas, to start growing their economies. The book sheds light on issues like spending too much on the military and the harm caused by monopolies and corruption. It also focuses on how building patriotism, national pride, and good government can help societies improve. Each chapter builds on the one before it, making the book easy to follow and understand. The author covers topics like starting small local businesses, improving schools, using new ideas and technology, and protecting the environment. This shows readers a complete plan for how to help countries grow and succeed.

Language

The book uses simple and clear language, which makes its important ideas easy for everyone to understand. Even though the topics are serious and need deeper thinking, the way it is written helps people from different educational backgrounds follow along. The sentences are short and straightforward, and the author explains things clearly without using complicated words. The book gives real-life examples, quotes from famous people, and stories from history to make the points more believable and relatable. These examples help the readers connect with the ideas and see how they might work in their own lives. The author also uses comparisons and simple stories to explain hard ideas about the economy and government in a way that anyone can understand. By keeping the language simple and avoiding confusing terms, the book makes it easier for readers to imagine how they can use these ideas in their own communities. It also helps readers feel confident that they can learn and apply these ideas, no matter where they are starting from. This approach makes the book useful for a wide range of people, including students, teachers, community leaders, and even government officials.

Relatability to the Target Audience

The ideas in the book are important for everyone, but they are especially meaningful for people in developing countries. It talks about real problems like scarcity, exploitation, unstable régimes, and damage to the environment. The book shows how these issues affect millions of people in their daily lives. Sellama also explains how not having good schools and bad leadership can keep a country from growing. These are problems that many developing nations face, and the book talks about them in great detail. The book doesn't just highlight the problems; it gives real solutions that people can use to make things better. This makes readers feel hopeful and helps them believe they can make a difference. It shows that everyone has a role to play and that by working together, communities can solve big problems. The book encourages readers to think of themselves as part of the solution and inspires them to take action to help their country move forward. By talking about both the struggles and the solutions, the book creates a connection between ideas and real life. It reminds readers that progress happens when people work together and take responsibility for making change happen. This makes the book inspiring and practical for anyone who wants to help improve their community or country.

Similar Books

Readers who enjoyed works like *Beating the Odds: Jump-Starting Developing Countries* by Justin Yifu Lin or *Turnaround: Third World Lessons for First World Growth* by Peter Blair Henry will find a similar depth of insight and inspiration in Mahfoud B. Sellama's **The Economic Prescription** for Developing Countries.

Beating the Odds: Jump-Starting Developing Countries: his book explores how poor countries can ignite economic growth without waiting for global action or ideal local conditions. It challenges conventional wisdom and provides practical strategies for development.

Turnaround: Third World Lessons for First World Growth: Henry discusses lessons that developed nations can learn from the economic policies of developing countries. He emphasizes the importance of discipline and pragmatic policy choices in achieving growth.

How Nations Escape Poverty: Zitelmann examines the economic transformations of countries like Poland and Vietnam, highlighting the role of capitalist growth and entrepreneurial reforms in escaping poverty.

These comparisons underscore Sellama's distinctive perspective while placing *The Economic Prescription for Developing Countries* within a broader framework of impactful works on economic growth and transformation. Readers who appreciate the practical insights and inspiring strategies in titles like *Beating the Odds* or *Turnaround* will discover equally compelling ideas and solutions in this book.

Recommendations

The Economic Prescription for Developing Countries is an important book with great ideas that can help improve the lives of people in developing nations. Given its relevance and practical insights, it is imperative to market this book extensively in developing countries. Social media is a great way to spread the word about this book. It can help reach different types of people like teachers, government leaders, activists, and regular citizens who want to make their communities better. The book talks about how countries can become independent by focusing on their own strengths, using new ideas, and protecting the environment. These are things that governments, non-profit groups, and community leaders will find very helpful.

To make sure the book helps as many people as possible, it should be marketed widely through online platforms. Books like this are always useful because they give ideas that can help for a long time and start important conversations about making things better. By reaching lots of people, this book can inspire positive changes and encourage communities to work together for a better future. Adding more detail, this book gives clear steps for improving economies, like creating more jobs, focusing on education, and using technology to solve problems. It also talks about how countries can work together and share ideas to grow stronger. If it is promoted the right way, this book can be a powerful tool to help many countries move forward and improve their citizens' lives.

Contents

Introduction

It is believed that development results from the availability and use of factors of production such as land, labor, capital, and entrepreneurs. However, sometimes these factors alone are insufficient to launch an economy or spur development in countries that lack either economic direction or a firm political decision to progress from point A to point B. Some countries lack both, making it exceedingly difficult to even begin.

In today's world, some countries possess only a few of these production factors and lack the rest, which again complicates the achievement of industrialization. It is important to remember that even if a country possesses all these factors, it cannot achieve development without a serious government committed to taking rigorous steps forward. An economic and political decision is essential to launch an "Economic Revolution."

This book discusses the persistent underdevelopment in many countries. It will suggest ideas on how to create economic and political infrastructure, generate jobs, enhance production, improve education and customer service, and increase national income. To offer remedies for launching an economic revolution, we must address the multiple, complex causes behind the stagnation of developing countries.

The book is written in simple language to ensure it is accessible to people of different languages and educational levels. It serves as a summary of straightforward economic strategies that lay the groundwork for a more sophisticated economy.

Poverty in Developing Countries

Many people wonder whether poverty is preordained or is due to different challenging circumstances. According to Nelson Mandela, Poverty is man-made, just like slavery. He argued that governments are behind the poor living conditions of any person. "There is no such thing as a poor country, only a failing government that does not know how to distribute wealth adequately," Noam Chomsky said.

Some thinkers believe that the North wants to keep the South as it is. In other words, the North wants to keep the South as "The breadbasket for the North." In this arrangement, the South supplies the North with natural resources, such as oil, gas, iron, uranium, steel, gold, diamonds, and wood, in exchange for processed products such as medicines, machines, tools—and sometimes food. Certain developing countries provide the North with cheap fruits and vegetables, such as the case of Mexico, Chile, and Brazil, providing resources to the United States and such as the case of North African countries to South Europe.

The South has found itself stuck in a deep dependency on necessities coming from the North in exchange for everything precious they have. Most leaders in developing countries think that providing all the necessary resources for the North is the fastest and most efficient way to secure the support of Northern leaders. They do so because they expect leaders in the North to help them and their families acquire the right to reside in the North once they retire.

According to Xavier Driencourt, a French ambassador to North Africa, "Some leaders and officials of Developing Countries beg for visas for their kids to go to study in the North." The children will eventually settle in the North and tend to the properties and money their fathers transfer to the North while in power.

Although millions of citizens complain about this dependency, it's always in vain. Leaders in some developing countries have established a culture that has made the success of their economies dependent on the North.

Political Instability

Political stability is very important for the economic development of a country. A country that goes through a continuous change in governments or in officials can never launch an economy. A government needs stability in order to focus on its projects and what needs to be done in every field.

In addition, a country that goes through a civil war, for instance, will never have the time, energy, or money to move forward because the focal point is on the war and never the economy. Unfortunately, many developing countries find themselves caught in civil war at one time or another. A civil war, as we know, can drag on for years and exact enormous tolls in terms of lives, money, and infrastructure.

Citizens, at this point, should have the ultimate say in expressing their desire to call all militias or guerillas (or whatever they are called in that country) to stop the fight. It is in everybody's interest to focus on fixing the economy and bringing the country back on track. Citizens have the right to live their lives and fulfill their dreams. They don't want to be caught in the middle of a conflict between two governments or two parties challenging one another.

I was born in a developing country, and I know that every citizen has simple dreams: to have a job, a house, a family, a car, and especially stability.

Almost every human being believes that politics is a dirty game. Another common belief is that, unlike other games, politics has no rules. Unfortunately, when said human takes office, he forgets that saying. Power, money, lust, and prestige will take over that human and turn him against his species. It is said that humans are the only species that hate and kill each other. A lion never kills another lion, and a dog never kills another dog.

Political stability is essential for economic stability. However, the opposite can cause the country to lose all quality of life and all the means for survival. Political instability took many countries hundreds of years behind. People lost everything they had, everything they worked for, almost all their loved ones, and especially their dreams. Perhaps at the end of the conflict, people would wonder whether that particular war was necessary. When World War II ended, people asked an interesting question: "What was that all about?" We have to bear in mind that it would be extremely difficult to start an economy after a period of civil war!

The West and Developing Countries

Many people in developing countries blame the West or rich countries for their poverty. They think that these rich countries are taking their resources almost for free to develop, leaving them with no means of producing goods and services.

Some claim that their governments are accomplices to the West in keeping them poor. Some leaders are accused of serving the West in return for rights of residence for themselves and their families. In addition to this, many resent the West for allowing some leaders to transfer millions of dollars to Western banks easily without asking them about the origin of these fortunes. In the US, for instance, if a person deposits more than $10,000, the government has the right to ask for the origin of that money; it might originate from money laundering or other nefarious practices. France is another example that has strict laws when it comes to deposits by citizens. Citizens cannot deposit more than 1000 Euros for fear that the government will ask them for the origin of that money. Ironically, both countries allow the transfer of millions of dollars into personal accounts by leaders from developing countries without asking for the origin of that money.

Some citizens of developing countries think that the West is using their soils as breadbaskets to feed its people. Because of the cost of the production of fruits, vegetables, cereals, and other produce, the West prefers to buy these crops from breadbasket countries for a few dollars. Since crops are cheap in dollars, and since peasants or farmers in developing countries make an average of $0.65 to $ 2 a day, the cost then is minimal, and the profit is huge. The same practices occur with the production of clothes, machines, tools, fabrics, and other items. Therefore, many plants were moved to developing countries because of the cheap cost and huge profits.

Corruption

Corruption, the economic cancer, has consumed all aspects of life in developing countries and contributed to the poverty of millions. Regrettably, the label of corruption is often automatically associated with the leaders of these countries; when asked about the causes of poverty there, many point directly to corruption. Sadly, there are officials who seem to care only about their own and their families' well-being.

It is a well-known fact in some nations that high-ranking officials siphon money directly from the treasury, skim off the revenues from natural resources such as diamonds and gold, or secure bank loans that they never intend to repay.

Some ministers or cabinet members, lacking direct access to the treasury, may purposely sabotage the production of certain goods or the cultivation of specific grains, fruits, and vegetables. This creates market shortages, allowing them to import these items from the North, thus cleverly and connivingly siphoning money. For instance, these officials might target farms producing essential commodities to strike opaque deals to buy these products and alleviate the shortages. Once a suitable farm is identified, they make an offer to the manager. Given the scale of the purchase— intended to meet the demands of an entire nation—the farmer often agrees to the deal, which guarantees significant and sustained business for his farm. So far, everything may seem above board. However, the malpractice occurs when the officials insist that the farmer deposit any commissions directly into their personal bank accounts, rather than into the national treasury. Moreover, these officials consistently fail to report these commissions to their superiors. If a farmer declines the deal, suspecting foul play with government funds, the officials simply continue their search until they find a compliant partner.

Secondly, some officials seek out farmers who can supply items that are deliberately made scarce—again, to facilitate importation for personal gain. In these more devious schemes, the officials ask the farmer to inflate the bill and deposit the difference into their personal account. For example, suppose a kilogram of tomatoes costs $2 on European farms, and the nation requires about 3 million tons for the year. An official might instruct the farmer to list $3 per kilogram on the receipt. If the farmer agrees, he would issue a receipt for $9 million instead of $6 million, and the $3 million difference would be deposited into the official's personal bank account. Should the farmer refuse, suspecting governmental fraud, the official would continue searching for another farmer willing to comply with this corrupt arrangement. This pattern repeats whenever any item is in shortage, demonstrating the extent of funds these officials divert for personal enrichment.

These practices extend to other essential purchases such as medical equipment for hospitals, machinery for factories, weapons for the military, and aircraft for airlines. If all officials engage in such behavior, the country could lose millions, if not billions, of dollars, leading to the closure of farms and factories and massive layoffs, as the government imports everything. Most people in developing countries are aware of these corrupt dealings but feel powerless to stop them due to fear of official retaliation and the scale of the corruption.

Ironically, governments in developing countries often blame their citizens for being lazy and careless, employing a tactic described by Noam Chomsky: "In order to control people, make them believe they are the cause of their own poverty and misery." Additionally, beleaguered governments tend to believe that everyone is conspiring against them. Conversely, citizens accuse their leaders of corruption and a lack of genuine interest in improving national well-being. They also criticize their governments for continually purchasing weapons solely to suppress any uprisings, perceiving no external threat—only governmental hostility towards its own people. This cycle of mutual accusations escalates daily, bringing the situation to a boiling point that seems inevitably destined to explode. It is only a matter of time before each country reaches its tipping point.

As a conclusion, in order to combat corruption, a serious government must ensure all its imports and exports are analyzed by parliament. Nothing should be purchased without parliamentary approval. Additionally, it is crucial to establish committees at all levels to monitor every purchase and transaction to prevent financial leaks, which can severely damage the economy, especially in a country with weak economic infrastructure and negligible oversight. Lastly, parliament should enact stringent laws that punish anyone who misappropriates government funds, treating such actions as a federal crime with severe consequences.

Military Spending in Developing Countries

Developing countries often purchase substantial amounts of military equipment from the North due to fears of potential wars or aggression. They prefer to live in fear rather than seek peace. While not suggesting a complete halt in weapon purchases, it would be advisable for these countries to invest more in improving their economies to enhance the well-being of their citizens instead of spending excessively on arms. Making peace with potential adversaries is often a better, faster, and less expensive solution than waging war or accumulating weapons, which deprives citizens of essential resources for survival. In some cases, countries have funds for weaponry but lack the means to buy food or medicine for their people. Many citizens believe their governments acquire such armaments solely to suppress them in the event of protests or uprisings concerning economic conditions.

Learning from the experiences of Japan and Germany post-World War II could prove beneficial. Both nations, having been stripped of their military capabilities, redirected their investments from military spending to economic development.

Today, Germany boasts the strongest economy in Europe, and Japan holds the third-largest economy globally. Japan maintains a military force of approximately 247,000 active personnel in a country of 125 million people, while Germany has about 181,000 military personnel in a nation of 83 million. Similarly, South Africa, with a population of 59 million, maintains just over 40,000 soldiers on active duty, choosing not to allocate excessive funds to military expenditures.

In today's world, warfare has become more sophisticated than ever before, and size does not determine power. Billions can be spent on military capabilities, yet an enemy could still target crucial survival resources using undetectable drones. They could strike gas and oil fields, electricity plants, and water dams or even contaminate drinking water with deadly viruses or biological agents, posing a significant threat to the populace.

This type of war would not last months or days but merely a few hours. With today's drone technology, even aircraft carriers are vulnerable and face significant danger. Countries spend billions of dollars to build these carriers and equip them for extended voyages, yet just a couple of drones can cause them to sink.

Therefore, "it is in the self-interest of countries to prepare for peace rather than for war." It is better to invest all that money in technology, research, agriculture, or at least in small industries such as cars, TVs, fridges, washing machines, and cell phone manufacturing, and make people's lives easier rather than spending billions on military equipment.

Bureaucracy

Bureaucracy is another stumbling block in many developing countries. An excessive amount of paperwork is required for even the smallest tasks. For instance, to open a small business, the city or sometimes even the federal government requires a multitude of documents and photographs to complete a "dossier." This dossier might include your birth certificate, your parents' birth certificates, proof of residence, your photographs, your blood type, a background check, a document confirming you don't own another business, proof of tax status, employment status, and notably, proof that you consistently vote. To apply for housing, forget it—you would need pounds of legal documents. A standard "dossier" might take weeks to prepare for a citizen, and if it's for housing, a business, or even a passport, it could take months. Often, people abandon their projects because of the overwhelming number of documents required, some of which are nearly impossible to obtain. Some don't even attempt their projects, knowing the time and hassle involved in gathering all the necessary paperwork.

The purpose of these documents is often unclear, though officials claim they are necessary to prevent fraud and cheating. In reality, most fraud occurs at higher levels by top officials and can cost the country millions of dollars. In the US, similar processes or paperwork would take just a few days. For example, to apply for a passport, all you need is your birth certificate, two photographs, an application, and a service fee. Perhaps just a couple of hours are sufficient to complete such a task. Moreover, you don't always have to visit the designated office in person; you can simply mail the paperwork to the office and wait a couple of weeks to receive your passport at home.

The application asks for your name, date of birth, place of birth, gender, address, and where to send the completed passport—that's it! To deter fraud in the US, the application form includes a legal notice at the bottom. It warns applicants against lying or committing any type of fraud, stating that such actions could result in a $5,000 fine and six months in jail. Reading this warning, an applicant is likely to think twice about the information they provide. This method of acquiring a passport is not only efficient but also effective in preventing fraud. The same technique is applied across various departments; each application form includes a specific legal warning urging the applicant to provide truthful information or face legal consequences. It's worth noting that in the US, most departments only require your ID, which suffices for identification purposes, reducing paperwork, saving time and money, and minimizing hassle.

Customer service in most departments in many developing countries is deplorable. Often, clerks are minimally educated or entirely uneducated, treating citizens poorly and making them wait for hours. Endless queues form for seemingly unnecessary documents, such as birth certificates. Knowing the desperate need of the citizens for these documents, some clerks won't hesitate to expect bribes to expedite the process. Complaints about such treatment typically fall on deaf ears, with no progress made in acquiring the necessary documents. This constitutes a form of subtle abuse; it is degrading and detrimental to the quality of life.

Customer service has long degraded the quality of life, perpetuating poor conditions because no one complains or listens. When complaints go unheard, all services and amenities remain poor, outdated, and often unacceptable. Effective customer service is essential for enhancing citizens' quality of life.

Inflation and High Prices

Prices in developing countries are perpetually unstable. In some places, prices fluctuate daily. Failing governments often fail to provide a convincing explanation to their citizens. Occasionally, they blame certain businessmen and factory owners for speculating and gouging prices merely to distract from the government's inability to provide goods and services at reasonable prices. Many businesspeople have been unjustly imprisoned as the governments seek to justify their shortcomings.

To reduce prices, there is only one theory and one solution: produce, produce, and produce! In other words, a country must have plenty of factories to produce all types of goods and services. The number of factories, assemblies, plants, and administrations should be proportional to the population. Therefore, to keep prices down, these plants and factories should operate continuously. By definition, when supply is high, prices will automatically fall. However, if production is absent, demand will surpass supply, and prices will continue to rise. For example, if farmers produce a surplus of every type of fruit and vegetable annually, supply will exceed demand, and consequently, prices will decrease. Now, citizens can afford to buy what they need for just a few dollars. As a result, the value of the currency will increase—for instance, $10 might buy food for a whole week. Therefore, people will have extra money for other inexpensive items, feeling that their money has substantial purchasing power. Thus, the government won't need to print money frequently because people have surplus funds. Now, considering the purchasing power of $10, imagine what $100 could do. At the end of the day, someone earning

$500 a week would feel relatively affluent.

When people have extra money, they tend to spend it on other goods, needs, wants, services, and even leisure, all of which are available domestically. The more money they spend, the more mines, farms, factories, plants, and assembly lines keep producing goods and services. The more goods and services produced, the more people will retain their jobs. The whole cycle is like a chain; everything is interconnected. If one part of the chain fails, the entire system will be affected.

The government can also play a role by encouraging half the population to produce and the other half to shop incessantly. Through media, commercials, and national propaganda, the government can educate people about this economic cycle, encouraging them to both produce and consume extensively to maintain general happiness.

If a country produces more than it needs, the surplus can be used for barter, exports, or preserved for future contingencies such as wars, droughts, famines, or national security concerns.

If a country continuously imports goods, food, and services, the result will be extremely costly. Importing everything means having no mines, no factories, no farms—and as a result, citizens won't have jobs, creating a significant burden on the government. Citizens will become increasingly unhappy, and anger will grow daily. Eventually, the government will face two choices: either support those without jobs financially or confront an angry population, potentially leading to a revolution. Either option is costly, so it is in the government's best interest to build as many factories, clean millions of acres of farming land, and dig as many mines as possible to provide jobs for the unemployed. A wise government would opt to build everything, which likely costs the same or less than supporting unemployed young men.

Some countries, such as Algeria, have given large loans and donations to young people to start small businesses. Most of these businesses failed due to lack of experience, lack of an economic vision, or because they entered markets unsuitable for them. However, these countries would have been better off using those funds to build factories and plants, providing jobs for the unemployed. This approach would have been quicker, cheaper, and more effective. Moreover, such quick solutions would only keep that generation busy for a short time, whereas building factories and assembly lines would benefit that generation and those to follow.

To maintain a healthy economy with low inflation, less printed money, a high value of the national currency, and strong consumer purchasing power, the extensive production of goods is the only sustainable solution and key to survival.

Distraction

Some governments in developing countries have become adept at distracting their citizens to keep them unaware or uninformed about what goes on behind the scenes in politics, economics, and social issues. Soccer has become the ultimate tool for distraction, to the extent that some countries now harbor animosity towards each other over game outcomes. Soccer has taken on a significance greater than religion in many societies. This tactic of distracting citizens was first initiated by the Roman Empire when things were not going well for the citizens of Rome. Caesar began a series of gladiator competitions to keep the Romans distracted and oblivious to their economic and social welfare. An Egyptian scholar, Mr. Gezzali, remarked, "I am surprised at people screaming and crying over the loss of a soccer game but not crying over the loss of their countries and civilizations."

Soccer is just a 90-minute distraction from our daily lives. It has not ended world poverty, nor has it helped children gain access to food, healthcare, or education. Soccer has never stopped wars, military conflicts, genocides, or the influx of refugees who leave everything precious behind. It has never ended human rights violations or spread democracy. According to Noam Chomsky, "the best defense against democracy is to distract people." Some governments in developing countries now look for any way to distract their citizens to make them forget their problems and misery. Some have even resorted to providing drugs of all kinds just to maintain order, hoping it will last.

Governments in developing countries often blame the West for the demise and misery their people endure, which is another type of distraction. They frequently invoke old colonialism, world imperialism, and an ever-watchful enemy—always seeking excuses to cover their failures and shirking responsibility. These governments have not taken the initiative to emulate the West in aspects where it excels and how it improves the lives of its citizens. Some leaders spend half the year in Western countries but never take steps to implement what they have seen and learned there. To them, the West is paradise, a paradise that should not be shared with anyone else.

Governments have become cunning in how they distract their citizens, so they do not pay attention to politics or the economy. For example, they create shortages of necessary goods and services, resulting in people spending excessive time talking, worrying, and scrambling to obtain these items. Sometimes, they stand in long queues just to buy essentials like a loaf of bread, cooking oil, or a carton of milk.

Deforestation/Desertification and Planting

Planting millions, if not billions, of trees is the way forward; it provides more food, more oxygen, and better protection for our environment. Millions of acres of trees have been depleted for various reasons; lumber companies cut thousands, if not millions, of trees annually. It is reported that Central Africa loses an area three times the size of New Jersey in trees every year. Additionally, millions of trees are destroyed by fires every season, and many more are used by impoverished people who lack gas for cooking. The lack of cooking gas and sometimes high prices have led thousands, if not millions, of poor people to cut trees; consequently, some regions have become arid or turned into deserts. In some areas, the demand for firewood has driven the cost of a bushel to over a hundred dollars. For instance, in the Republic of Congo, 90% of families use charcoal for cooking. According to enoughproject.org, the demand for charcoal in the Congo has led to the formation of cartels that produce and sell firewood, resulting in militias fighting for control over certain regions, including Africa's oldest national park. The Republic of Congo is not the only country heavily reliant on charcoal; many others are similarly dependent but to varying degrees. Haiti is another country that relies on charcoal for cooking; according to blogsworldbank.org, 80% of urban households use charcoal as their primary cooking fuel. My Haitian students report that the country now has almost no trees due to the demand for charcoal.

The extensive burning of trees for charcoal might be the second or third main reason for the depletion of the ozone layer, a major global concern. To combat this issue, it is imperative for governments in developing countries to plant as many trees as possible as soon as possible. This is an easy process but requires significant effort and serious political and economic decisions. Governments must educate their citizens about the economic, social, and environmental dangers caused by the lack of trees using every available means of media, communication, and billboards. They should motivate their citizens to volunteer to plant as many trees as can be planted and protect these precious resources. Governments can also enlist the help of military personnel to plant trees. It is a matter of survival for some countries; therefore, it should be a national endeavor.

As an example, Ethiopia, a developing country that is making significant progress, recently completed the Green Legacy Initiative. On July 29th, the government inspired all citizens to participate in a one-day tree-planting event with the goal of planting 200 million tree seedlings. Surprisingly, within 12 hours, the motivated citizens exceeded the target, planting over 350 million seedlings—an astonishing achievement that demonstrates to other nations the feasibility of such projects with sufficient commitment. According to BBC.com, the Labor Party has pledged to plant 2 billion trees by 2040.

China is another model for planting billions of trees for economic and environmental reasons. According to Time magazine, the Chinese president pledged to plant 70 billion trees as part of his commitment to the slogan "Green Our Planet," aimed at increasing forest carbon sinks and combating climate change.

A brilliant and encouraging initiative was taken by Nepal—a landlocked country in South Asia—some years ago. As a form of tax, the plan required every tourist to either personally plant a tree or sponsor one, contributing to environmental protection. The Ministry of Tourism adopted the slogan "Tourism Responding to the Challenge of Climate Change," a smart way to motivate people and involve every concerned individual.

Desertification

Desertification, or the advance of the desert, has been an ongoing phenomenon in several countries, particularly in regions close to deserts. Due to drought and desert storms, thousands of miles of fertile land have turned into deserts. The Republic of Algeria has suffered tremendously from this. In the late '60s and early '70s, Algeria was perhaps the first country in the world to take steps to stop desertification with a project called "The Green Dam." According to lejournaldelafrique.com, the government planted 370 million seedling trees across 3 million hectares. The main objective was to combat desertification and to protect its flora, agriculture, and water tables.

Today, it is crucial for every developing country in the world to combat deforestation and desertification and embark on tree planting. It should be a matter of national pride and a call to action to provide a better environment and a cleaner Earth for ourselves, our children, and future generations.

The Danger of Dependency on the North

Although most developing countries possess all types of factors of production, sometimes by the millions of tons, they can't even produce "a needle." Everything they need comes from the North. Gradually, this dependency has led to stagnation and underdevelopment in every sector. Jobs have become scarce, unemployment is rising sharply, inflation is through the roof, and buying power has plummeted. All of this will likely lead to unrest in many developing countries in the years to come.

It is urgent to recognize the danger of the living conditions of the millions of people in these countries. This will, sooner or later, lead to a massive exodus toward the North. It is only a matter of time. Thousands of men, women, and children from Africa are crossing the Mediterranean Sea as we speak.

Unfortunately, some of these young people never make it to the other side. Dozens of bodies are currently floating in the Mediterranean Sea, as most of these boats are cheaply made, some even from plastic, and cannot withstand the rough waves.

The lack of jobs, housing, and almost everything one can dream of is pushing every person to consider crossing borders and seas. It is time for world leaders to act and seek solutions to prevent these potential exoduses toward the North, which would strain and possibly cripple its economies. Financial aid, food aid, loans, and gifts to developing countries or bribes to their leaders have not solved the problem. It is often said, "Do not give a man a fish every day; instead, teach him how to fish." International organizations have been aiding developing countries for decades, but this help has only provided short-term sustenance. Now, these nations are back to square one. These organizations should have taught the people how to grow food, build infrastructure, and start small businesses instead of merely feeding them.

Private Ownership Can Be Bad for the Economy

Sometimes, private ownership is harmful to the economy due to its monopolistic nature at almost all levels. For instance, in the case of fruits and vegetables, many farmers intentionally produce limited quantities or control the production of certain items to keep prices high and maximize profits. This is also true for farmers who produce white and red meat, and dairy products, who deliberately keep production low to maintain high prices.

The same strategy is applied by fishermen who catch only a certain amount of fish to keep prices high. They do not exert effort to catch more, content with catching just enough to ensure substantial profits. Thus, when a customer goes to buy fish or shrimp, the fisherman claims, "There is hardly any fish in the ocean, and that's all I have," which justifies the high prices. Consequently, customers find themselves paying exorbitant prices for seafood.

To address this issue, the government should intervene in two ways:

Regulate prices to a level that consumers can afford. However, this may lead producers to reduce their output further or exit the market entirely, leaving consumers struggling to find the fruits, vegetables, fish, or other products they need and desire.

In situations like these, it is often beneficial for governments to own the means and places of production. Unlike private speculators who are driven by greed and disregard the purchasing power of citizens, governments typically consider the well-being of their populace.

The government needs to own its farms and factories to compete with speculators who aim to make a substantial profit in a short period by controlling market supply. Competition between government goods and those offered by private owners will keep speculators honest, prevent them from exploiting consumers, and help maintain prices at a level most citizens can afford.

Monopoly is Bad for the Economy

Monopoly means that a person or a company is allowed to invest in a specific type of business, goods, or services but does not permit any other entity to enter the same market. This company aims to produce certain products without competition and eventually sells these products, however, wherever, and whenever it wants.

In some developing countries, wealthy individuals or certain businessmen and entrepreneurs request exclusivity from their government, making them the sole producers, exporters, or importers of certain goods and services. This concept is very harmful to the economy of that country. It is understandable if someone, after hard work and research, invents something new and beneficial to society and wants a patent to be the only producer. However, if it involves a common product or an imported item, and many entrepreneurs wish to enter the same market, then the government should allow anyone to participate. Ultimately, consumers will benefit from this non-exclusivity approach. This theory would otherwise inhibit the efforts and energy of other entrepreneurs to provide the same goods and services.

Remember, more supply means more reasonable prices that consumers can afford. The government should encourage more entrepreneurs to enter the same markets so that competition and multiple efforts provide more and better goods and services.

Developing countries' governments are sometimes incapable of providing things to consumers for various reasons. At times, it is the high population that creates substantial demand, necessitating a significant supply. Sometimes, it is due to the lack of money, lack of necessary tools, the right people to manage operations, a good transportation network, or other preoccupations. If governments want peace of mind, they should encourage and allow more entrepreneurs to enter any market and reject the theory of exclusivity, along with the laws supporting it.

Monopoly would lead to fewer goods and services in the market and higher prices for multiple wants and needs in societies. Entrepreneurs can exploit this concept to control the production, sale, import, or export of certain items to raise prices and make exorbitant profits. As an economic remedy, government involvement is crucial.

Taxes

People all over the world dislike taxes, but educated individuals understand that taxes are necessary for building a nation and its economy. Taxes have existed for thousands of years. The first record of taxation in ancient Egypt dates back about 5000 years when the Pharaoh collected the equivalent of 20% of the harvest in taxes. Similarly, the old Asian Feudal System allowed emperors to collect substantial taxes from peasants in the form of crops. Today, developed countries rely heavily on taxes to build and maintain infrastructure and provide education, healthcare, and other major services for their citizens. Governments also use taxes to pay for the multiple services rendered by federal employees. Unfortunately, in many developing countries, people, businessmen, and even officials refuse to pay taxes. They often find ways to avoid paying them or do not pay the correct amount they owe to their governments. As a result, governments in developing countries struggle to pay their bills and their debts, and take care of their citizens. They even struggle to provide the minimum services for their citizens and have little money to build new infrastructure or repair existing buildings, roads, highways, and public spaces.

Not paying taxes means that governments must raise the prices of everything. For instance, if a government of a country needs $500 billion yearly to function properly, and it collects only $350 billion, there is a shortage of $150 billion. This shortfall occurs because some businesses, wealthy individuals, and officials do not pay taxes. It is noteworthy that presidents and officials in these countries often do not pay taxes, believing they are exempt, unlike in the United States, where presidents and officials must pay taxes—a great role model for others to follow. To compensate for the $150 billion shortfall, the government must raise the prices of many goods and services. Consequently, in developing countries today, the prices of food and services are higher than in developed countries. Meat, fish, and poultry have become luxuries. Land, property, and businesses cost more in developing countries than in developed ones. It might take a person their entire life to save enough money to buy a house or an apartment or half their life to afford a new car. If the trend of not paying the correct taxes continues annually, the prices of goods and services will keep rising, leading to catastrophic inflation and driving millions into poverty.

Governments in developing countries need to educate their citizens about the importance of taxes for building the economy, funding services, and repairing infrastructure like roads, bridges, schools, and hospitals—thereby ultimately creating jobs. Officials also have an obligation to pay taxes themselves to set an example for the rest of the population.

Education about paying taxes should not be limited to TV debates and radio channel discussions; it should also be incorporated into school curricula. Students of all disciplines should study economics, the laws of supply and demand, and global economies. They should be educated about taxes and the economy of their country to understand the importance of taxes and how these contribute to their future. By doing so, governments will be able to nurture new generations with a robust understanding of the economy and how to enhance it. In the US, high schools teach economics, political science, and even law, with chapters dedicated to teaching students about taxes, international trade, currencies, and globalization. Ultimately, this education will help governments build one of the most crucial elements in forming a perfect society: responsible citizens.

Freedom of the Press is Also Good for the Economy

To keep a watchful eye on the economy, the performance of mayors, governors, government officials, and all commercial and federal institutions, the government should ensure the freedom of the press. Freedom of the press is a powerful tool that can drive societies towards improvement. Often, the president or his cabinet may be unaware of what is happening in every city, town, and village. Concerned journalists would visit these places, talk to the citizens, and uncover the problems they face. The government has bigger issues to address than investigating every local issue, making journalists crucial in ensuring that citizens live right and dignified lives. A good life today means having a job, a house, access to education, healthcare, clean water, and overall safety. Unfortunately, most of these rights are unavailable in many developing countries, where citizens cannot even enjoy a decent life.

Journalists can report cases of fraud, shady activities, and transactions, or anything that might harm the country's economy. A free press would keep every administration and institution on the right track. Honesty and excellent service should be the motto of every institution in any country. In the case of developing countries, journalists can also be tasked with monitoring the performance of agriculture, industry, construction, and the production of certain sensitive products. Some products are critical for national security. In fact, many farms and plants have malfunctioned and defaulted because there was no oversight.

Journalists can also keep an eye on services rendered by government institutions and forces, where employees and officials think they are untouchable. In developed countries and free societies, journalism is considered the fourth estate. This means that journalists oversee everything, much like how the US Congress oversees everything, including the actions of the

29

president. Many developing countries do not recognize the importance of journalists; on the contrary, they restrict their activities and control what they write because some officials engage in questionable activities.

Journalists should be active throughout the country to ensure everything functions properly, at least giving the elected government some credibility and legitimacy.

Unfortunately, some developing countries use journalists to deceive citizens into believing that everything is going well so that citizens remain content with the status quo. This behavior has exacerbated social, economic, and educational issues, sometimes severely.

In the absence of journalists, social problems such as crime, drugs, prostitution, and even diseases can spread more easily. Therefore, before it's too late, journalists can help expedite solutions and save as many lives as possible.

Journalists can also report cases of abuse, whether by federal employees or private ones. They can expose instances of racism and poor treatment of people or minorities. In countries that respect their citizens, journalists report on the quality of service rendered by even the smallest company.

To improve conditions in developing countries, governments should broadly protect journalists and their work through laws and immunity, enabling them to perform their duties effectively. In the US, for instance, the First Amendment of the Constitution protects both freedom of speech and freedom of the press. When such protections are afforded to journalists, they can report on anything that affects citizens' health, social well-being, and any barriers to people living normal lives.

Theoretically and practically—to launch an effective economy—everything is feasible and achievable; I don't understand why it is difficult for developing countries to make serious decisions and improve!

The Opposition

Governments must accept that having an opposition is beneficial for the well-being of a nation and its future. The opposition is not there to overthrow the government or wage a real war against the sitting president; nothing is personal. Just the presence of the opposition itself serves as a reminder to those in office that the country undergoes elections and that their term will eventually end. This deters any sitting president from attempting to change the constitution in his favor to remain in power indefinitely.

It is in human nature to be satisfied with one's way of life, methods, thinking, and vision for the future. However, when an individual senses that someone is watching, they are often motivated to strive for improvement. The same principle applies to governments monitored by an opposition. Even if the government in office is performing its duties, the presence of an opposition can spur it to do more to remain in power until the end of the term. The opposition is an effective institution that keeps the sitting government on track; otherwise, the government might take its time and act as it pleases, with no urgency.

The opposition vigilantly monitors every step and every law passed by the sitting government, serving as a crucial tool to correct wrongdoing and unseen actions. It identifies the mistakes of the government, holds it accountable, and suggests better solutions. Many governments have collapsed due to the absence of serious opposition—they thought they were heading in the right direction, but unfortunately, there was no one to correct their course. This is often the case in dictatorships, where leaders think they know better than their citizens until they reach a point where they can't even provide basic necessities like food.

"The absence of the opposition always leads to dictatorships."

Unfortunately, to maintain power, some unfit governments and leaders create a controlled opposition from within, pretending it was spontaneously formed to show international communities the appearance of democratic processes. This type of opposition often obeys the government and tries to convince citizens that the government's actions are beneficial. Some corrupt governments go so far as to appoint loyalists as heads of human rights offices. Consequently, the president of the Bureau of Human Rights defends all government actions and denies any abuses committed by the government.

Types of Economic Governments

If a state decides to adopt capitalism, it must adhere to all the rules and theories of capitalism. A country cannot selectively apply only those aspects it prefers because if the system fails, leaders and citizens may wrongly conclude that capitalism itself is inherently flawed.

You cannot have capitalism without competition, as competition is the foundation of innovation, beautification, and efficiency. It enables producers to offer goods and services at affordable prices, which in turn helps them to sell their products more easily and allows consumers to fulfill their needs and desires. Competition fosters the creation of better goods and services and ultimately leads to lower prices. Governments should allow competition and keep their hands off the market, as Adam Smith advocated. Sadly, in some developing countries, the government controls even the imports and exports of goods and services. This might be manageable in countries with small populations, but in nations with large populations, governments should allow anyone to enter the market. Governments should focus on other concerns instead. In the US, for instance—the leader in capitalism—the government primarily oversees the police and military forces, postal services, and public school teachers, while the private sector handles the rest of the businesses. The US grants freedom to businessmen to import and export everything except weapons and drugs. The government focuses on serious matters and avoids impeding business operations. Thus, governments in developing countries should encourage entrepreneurs to enter the markets and facilitate every step for these entrepreneurs to produce goods and services and make them available to customers at reasonable prices; this is their sacred mission!

You also can't have capitalism without the theory of supply and demand. Producers should flood the market with goods and services to ensure availability at all times. Sufficient or surplus supply will benefit consumers. Products will be accessible, and prices will remain reasonable. If supply is low, prices will rise, and customers will become unhappy. In such cases, the government should intervene to address the issue.

When goods and services are scarce or available in limited quantities, prices naturally increase. Customers may refrain from purchasing, which can slow down sales, production, transportation, and more. As a result, factories may struggle to sell their products at higher prices. Each time production lags, factory owners might lay off employees. It's a vicious cycle that should be monitored by specialists or committees. Sending workers home becomes a burden to the government. In other words, these workers will either pressure the government to create new jobs or will rely on welfare. Welfare is costly for any government; sometimes, governments need to seek loans from other countries. Therefore, it is in the government's self-interest to monitor the market to keep everyone satisfied.

I am in favor of governments owning significant corporations and farms and overseeing production. If the government owns lands and farms, it would be easier for food to be available at any time and place and at reasonable prices, at least to feed those who cannot afford to buy it.

Laissez-faire, laissez-passer is another component of capitalism. This means that governments should allow entrepreneurs to produce whatever they can, with no restrictions except, as previously mentioned, on producing guns and drugs. Aside from that, entrepreneurs can bring the best to societies. Governments know their citizens' needs and wants; in this case, the government can guide entrepreneurs on what to produce, how to produce, and for whom to produce.

It is in the best interest of any developing country trying to adopt capitalism to rigorously apply every theory to achieve the quantity and quality of economic outputs it needs. Government oversight of the economy is recommended because it is the only entity that genuinely cares about the people's welfare.

Socialism Is Good for Developing Countries

The Reasons for the Fall of Socialism

In theory, socialism benefits the citizens of any country. It provides jobs, housing, healthcare, social security benefits, maternity benefits, and protects bank deposits. This sounds ideal, except socialism has failed in many countries for several profound reasons, which led to the abandonment of this economic system. The collapse of socialism can be attributed to both political and practical reasons, but to me, it was not practiced as the socialist theorists envisioned.

For example, when land was divided among peasants or farmers in socialist countries, they were told what to produce, how to produce, and for whom to produce. Up to this point, everything seems well-conceived. However, those who tasked the farmers with production never monitored them or followed up.

Essentially, they gave them the land and the tools and then left them to their own devices, expecting production to happen. Additionally, the government never held any farmer accountable, which became a practical failure in every socialist country. The government should have conducted follow-ups, rewarding the best farmers or replacing them with more productive ones who cared about the quality of service. If farmers knew they could lose their land or be replaced, they would have been motivated to maintain their productivity.

The second reason for socialism's fall was political. Every capitalist country, especially during the Cold War, resented socialism and communism. The West criticized these systems, fearing they were taking over the world. The Soviet Union at the time was eager to convince other countries to adopt these systems, partly to spite the West. In response, the West fought hard to prevent the spread of this philosophy and started spreading news and propaganda, even in schools and universities, about the negative consequences of socialism and communism.

Millions came to believe that these systems were detrimental to people's well-being.

To me, if Russia had not tried to force other countries to adopt these systems during the inappropriate time of the Cold War, it could have focused on making socialism or communism successful and demonstrated to the world that these

ideologies could be beneficial for the well-being of any country. Many Western countries resented Russia and discouraged socialist countries from focusing on progress.

From this, we can conclude that now is an opportune time to implement socialism in developing countries to improve the lives of millions of citizens. Governments in these countries can clear land and divide it into large farms, allocating these fertile lands to specialized and serious farmers who care about their country's future. The leaders of these farms should be provided with all the necessary tools and funds to make the farms successful. These leaders should also receive incentives if they do a good job of producing ample food and services. They must understand that they can be replaced if they lose confidence or fail to meet the minimum production of goods and services needed to satisfy the market.

Governments should monitor production in every state. States should establish committees with specialists at the city and state levels to track the performance of these farms. Within a very short period, any country that adopts these techniques will significantly increase crop production to an unbelievable level. By doing so, they can satisfy the needs of local markets and begin exporting products to other countries or exchange them for items, goods, and services they lack.

Private Ownership of Land

Private ownership of land presents challenges. Landowners and farmers could control the quantities and prices of crops. Some landowners might one day decide to sell their lands for real estate development, resulting in the loss of significant portions of fertile land. Therefore, the national benefit should outweigh private benefits. To retain their lands, private landowners should contribute to the production of goods and services to meet every want and need of the citizens if they choose to.

Economic Dictatorship

It is ironic to suggest that an economic dictatorship could be beneficial for a country experiencing dire conditions or a sluggish economy. To elevate such a country from its plight, it would take an industrial revolution akin to the one in Europe in the 17th century or the current one in China. I am referring not to the political aspects but to the economic ones, which have dramatically reduced poverty, boosted economic growth, and elevated Chinese companies to some of the world's largest producers. For example, in 2022, 40% of goods and supplies imported into the US were from China. This is a testament to real economic development. China appears to be in a rush or in a race against time, seemingly striving to surpass the US and become the next superpower.

According to the Cato Institute, China is becoming "the perfect dictatorship." In other words, aggressive economic reforms can sometimes benefit a nation.

Implementing an aggressive plan means initiating a series of economic measures to push the economy forward at a rigorous rate. Perhaps this is what has led China to be so successful and daring enough to challenge any superpower.

Turkey is another example of a less aggressive form of economic dictatorship. In 1980, the country adopted new economic and liberal reforms; in other words, it made strong economic and political decisions to propel the country forward. Today, President Erdogan wants Turkey to be a developed country and aspires for it to be part of the European Union. According to the IMF, Turkey's GDP reached $905 billion in 2022. Turkey now boasts a mixed-market economy, making it the 19th largest economy in the world as of 2023. The country is a leader in producing motor vehicles, construction materials, agricultural products, textiles, transportation equipment, consumer electronics, and home appliances. Today, the United Nations classifies Turkey as a developed country after years of being considered developing. Turkey is also a member of the G20, an indicator of the country's rapid progress.

Turkey has even moved into producing military equipment and fighter jets, including the famous combat Bayraktar drone—one of the best remotely controlled drones that cost about $5 to $6 million each. Because of its high performance in the Russian-Ukrainian war—according to PBS.org—Kuwait has just struck a deal to buy these Turkish-made drones for $367 million, enough to secure jobs for the next ten years. According to Reuters, Saudi Arabia has also struck a similar deal with Turkey to purchase this combat drone. The sum was not disclosed, but it is believed to be the biggest defense contract that Turkey has ever secured. Such contracts can lead to the creation of thousands of jobs.

An economic dictatorship also requires all employees in every sector, whether private or governmental, to produce what consumers need. However, the private sector is often not concerned with customers' needs and wants; instead, they focus on producing goods and services that generate quick profits. It should be just like during the Second World War when the US government required the private sector and small factories to produce military supplies due to high demand.

In conclusion, we ought to say that in previous decades, any form of dictatorship was viewed as having negative effects on people and their countries. Today, the view has changed since China is doing well; somehow, this economic dictatorship is good for the well-being of the country, but I am not sure about the well-being of human rights. Thanks to the firm decisions of governments in both China and Turkey, they have transformed into strong nations with robust economies.

Perfect Government

In order to have a perfect government, a country needs a higher institution, such as Congress or Parliament, composed of many serious and devoted members. This institution should be the ultimate decider and hold all the power in the country; concentrated power in one person is a threat to the country, especially if this person came to power through a coup d'état or political struggle. For such a leader, one term in office is often not enough since they fought hard against the previous regime or other political parties. This leader might feel entitled to more terms, which in some countries can lead to 30 or 40 years in power. Often, such leaders may even consider passing power to one of their children.

A country should have at least three or four strong political parties, including labor and student parties. The traditional Democratic and Republican parties are somewhat outdated today and have lost credibility over time as they have not fulfilled their promises and have contributed to people's impoverishment.

Moreover, these parties do not represent the interests of workers and students, who are the backbone of a country, and rarely address their issues. These groups are often overlooked in political and social discussions, overshadowed by sports and music. Additionally, the inclusion of Progressive and technocratic parties is crucial as they can drive change and inspire hope and motivation.

Each city and state government should have a smaller version of the cabinet that includes departments such as economics, commerce, industry, agriculture, justice, public works, education, tourism, and cultural activities. The cabinets must include officials with degrees and expertise. Both cabinets and congressmen should coordinate with one another daily to ensure transparency and sincerity.

Each state should elect a state cabinet in the same disciplines to represent it in Parliament or Congress. Members must also be experts in their respective fields and possess higher education. Parliament should then include eight or ten representatives or congressmen from each state, in addition to a similar cabinet from each political party. This high institution would discuss matters and ultimately vote on laws and projects concerning the country. It is the supreme authority in the country.

The ruling party would need the approval of parliament to choose its cabinet members, including any generals, just like in the US. The president cannot appoint any high officials or ambassadors without the consent of Congress or Parliament.

If Parliament or Congress is not satisfied with the performance of the ruling government, it can hold a vote of no confidence and call for the election of a new government, just like in the UK. The vote of no confidence is an effective way to keep everyone accountable and not simply wait for the president's term to end to elect a new leader. It's inefficient for a country to wait four or five years each time a president performs poorly! Parliament or Congress could give the ruling government one more chance to rectify issues, but only once. Parliament oversees all military and enforcement forces and has the right to change all high-ranking officials within the military, navy, air force, and law enforcement. This prevents the country from becoming a military dictatorship.

The president should have a vice president, serving as a double-edged tool. First, if anything happens to the president, the vice president will carry out his duties.

Second, it prevents the president from becoming the sole decider, potentially becoming a dictator, or appointing a family member as a successor.

All laws and major projects must be analyzed by a special committee before even reaching the parliament floor. By doing so, any government must thoroughly consider its actions and projects.

This saves time and closes any loopholes for financial misappropriation or nepotism in awarding projects.

A major parliament committee should be formed by selecting the best cabinet members in the country to make decisions in case of deadlocks. It exists to review, listen to comments, receive criticism, and seek the best solutions for the interests of the citizens and the country.

Each member of Congress or Parliament should be elected for 5 years and limited to two terms. Long-serving congressmen can create lobbies; lobbies sometimes act as a soft dictatorship for corporations. The president should be elected for 4 or 5 years and also limited to two terms. The president must never have the power to change the constitution; this is solely parliament's duty.

A special building should be constructed in the capital to host parliament sessions. Additionally, a hotel should be built nearby to accommodate members when they are in town. Members should reside in their respective towns or cities until a session is called to avoid unnecessary expenditures. Members should stay in their cities to monitor ongoing projects and listen to citizens' concerns, as "out of sight, out of mind," as the saying goes.

The constitution of the country should be designed with the help of its citizens. Citizens should be involved in forming the laws of the land to foster a sense of responsibility and freedom. The constitution must outline the purpose, necessity, and multiple powers of "The Parliament" as the supreme institution of the country. Nothing should be done without parliament's approval. At the same time, Congressmen or parliament members should receive no immunity in cases of abuse of power or using their political position for personal advantage.

Political Decision

If a country realizes that things are really going bad, it becomes compulsory and urgent for the leader to halt everything and declare a new era. This new era involves a plan to change things not just for the better but for the best. A political decision is usually associated with a love for the country and doing whatever it takes to make it triumphant. Even if things are really bad, the leader must be honest with his people, and it is not shameful to ask for help to fix things together. Each country has thousands of intelligent people who can turn things around and push towards success. Thankfully, intelligence is not owned by any corporation or patented by any wealthy individual, otherwise, every poor country would remain poor forever.

The political decision is the key to success. If a leader makes such a decision, citizens will rally behind him to build their country together through hard work, devotion, and respect for each other, ultimately aiming for the stars. The leader should set a goal and announce his ambitions for the country to become as powerful as certain benchmarks, for his people to excel like others, and for future generations to have a better life.

The leader must also set measurable goals to make the country strong, powerful, self-reliant, and capable of producing everything its people need and want.

Some countries purposefully send students to the West to learn how to produce goods and services. Others send students to emulate the way of teaching, and managing healthcare and social affairs in Europe. Some countries send students to learn technology from other nations, while others have even sent spies to learn how to manufacture certain products. A government that wants to launch a new industrial revolution needs to undertake all these measures to be successful. Japan is a case in point; in the 1850s, when Commodore Matthew C. Perry led an expedition to Japan, the Japanese were appalled by the power of the new gunboats and realized how far behind they were compared to the

US. The emperor decided to end a

200-year policy of isolation and sent students to the US and Europe to study and learn about new inventions that were present at that time. This was a crucial political decision taken by the emperor of Japan to industrialize his country and modernize it.

Governments in developing countries should adopt the same political decision and embrace the vision that the Japanese emperor had. He transformed his country from a feudal and agricultural state into one of the best and most advanced countries in the world. Today, Japan has the third strongest economy in the world, after the US and China.

To encourage leaders in developing countries, it's noteworthy that Japan has one of the smallest amounts of natural resources in the world. Yet, due to determination and the right political decisions, Japanese engineers were able to acquire resources from other countries and then manufacture some of the best goods, tools, machines, cars, and computers, selling them to the rest of the world. It was once said that Japan used to buy heavy Russian cars, melt their iron and steel, and make two cars out of every Russian car. Through determination and hard work, a country can turn things around and become truly powerful and modern.

The Economic Decision is the Key

The government of any country must have a plan on how to fix the economy or how to start an efficient economy. The first step in executing this plan is to have the right people in the right places. Having the right people is essential for the success of any government and country at any time. Many countries have collapsed because of unfit leaders who were put in power either by inheritance, by force, or by deception. Running a country is not like running a store or daycare.

While running a store might not require education or specialization to sell basic products, running a country requires extensive knowledge, specialization, education, intelligence, and a clear vision for the future. Living and patching things up day by day is not the right way to fix a failing economy. To do this, a government should make 4- to 5-year plans, specifying what must be done to achieve these plans. Citizens prefer leaders who have clear plans and a visionary approach. These plans realistically show the leaders' interest, intelligence, intentions, and care for the citizens and the country.

Having a definite date and year for completing projects puts everyone on the same page and helps to fulfill the agenda embedded in the plan. Therefore, a leader must gather all resources and ensure that everyone in the cabinet works together to make promises a reality. It is better to set a definite date rather than an open one that workers and those in charge may not respect. To them, all projects will finish one way or another, so they see no rush. Unfortunately, this attitude is very common in most developing countries. It's a major reason for defaulting on numerous projects and postponing phases without clear reasons. Some projects move from one administration to another, some are never completed, and others are reported as completed only on paper. Every new government blames the previous one for slacking and not finishing the job, delaying many economically important projects that could have saved the country money and jobs.

Many leaders avoid this type of definitive planning, perhaps because they do not want to be held accountable for not fulfilling their projects and promises. I find these precise plans valuable because they can pressure the administration to accomplish everything on time. I believe that a job well done usually gives the leader the opportunity to be re-elected. In life, it is human nature to set up plans. For instance, someone might say, "By the end of next year, I will have saved

$20,000 to buy a car." Having such a plan is indeed a strategy for success. Success would also encourage that person to strive to save again for something bigger.

Ultimately, it would lead to a fulfilling sense of accomplishment and responsibility.

If each new government makes a 4 or 5-year plan, for example, the country will accomplish a lot because plans keep every resource and official focus on striving for excellence.

The economic decision is also meant to raise citizens' awareness of what needs to be done to move societies to higher standards and better directions. It also motivates citizens to participate, excel, and become leaders and role models for other nations. When a country completes Plan A, it can move to Plan B, then C, until the entire country is built in a well-organized manner in a short period of time. Working aimlessly never gets things done, and a lot of money is lost in the process, sometimes with no trace. Some officials like to operate in murky waters, and some want to be leaders but are unwilling to lead responsibly.

Forming Sub-Governmental Administrative Bodies

Sub-governmental administrative bodies should be formed at the city and state levels. For instance, each municipal city should establish a sub-governmental body similar to the national government. The mayor should form a cabinet akin to the one chosen by the president. Each sector should be managed by a specialist in that field, just like in the national or federal government. For example, there could be an official in charge of agriculture, another for industry, one for commerce, another for construction, one for education and health, and another for tourism. It is crucial to place the right person in the right role. The right person means someone who has a degree or experience in that field. When you have the right person in the right place, achievements become easier. Many developing countries suffer from the phenomenon of having the wrong person in the most sensitive sectors. Despite having plenty of intelligent and experienced individuals, they are often marginalized, according to most citizens.

The practice of a vote of no confidence, as carried out in some countries (especially the UK), is a valuable tool with which to maintain control and ensure accountability. It pressures city officials to work diligently and responsibly to fulfill citizens' needs and desires.

All city mayors and officials should be from the same state in which they serve. They understand their city and its intricacies, connect with its citizens, and know what needs to be done. An outsider would not possess this intimate knowledge. By the time an outsider familiarizes themselves with the city's neighborhoods and officials, their term could be over. Electing someone who lacks knowledge of the city they are supposed to manage is a common but unproductive practice in developing countries.

Similarly, governors must be from the state they govern and should be elected by the citizens of that state. Governors from other states might not care about the state they oversee; they may only look for projects that serve their personal interests before moving on to other states to repeat the process until they retire. This is a notorious issue among developing countries in how they govern their states. Some countries do not even allow citizens to choose their governors; instead, these officials are assigned by the federal government without consulting parliament.

Governors should also form a type of cabinet that includes officials who possess the same credentials in terms of specialty and experience required to perform such responsibilities. Each official will be in charge of the sector related to his specialty, the economy, agriculture, construction, education, health, etc., across the state.

Loss of confidence is necessary to keep everyone accountable for his or her performance. Poor performance of the cabinet should cost the governor and his cabinet their jobs.

Judges, sheriffs, and school district superintendents must also be from the same city they serve. Their election is crucial because accountability is one of the main factors contributing to the impoverishment of citizens in developing countries.

Even at the level of embassies, the government should assign people with specialties and experience in fields such as economy, agriculture, industry, education, and health. These individuals also have the duty to gather ideas on how the host countries manage various sectors. In other words, to report on the best ways and techniques in running businesses, banking, farming, education, and even culture.

Group Decisions

A perfect society or government should involve its people in every step to ensure everything functions well. Economic, educational, and political debates are healthy and valuable for the well-being of a country. At times, many decisions coming from the top are not accepted by the majority of citizens; that's why many of them are altered sooner or later. Forums are a good start on how to do things, improve things, or invent things. A perfect society would set up forums and conventions to study every sector and the reasons or causes of malfunctioning in that particular sector. Some governments in developing countries set up national meetings to discuss trivial matters as if they are major events. They should be focused on more pressing world and national security issues.

Farmers should gather in forums and conventions to discuss how to improve agriculture and how to use efficient ways to produce more crops. A minister of agriculture should not hold the position if he has never planted a tree in his life. The Ministry of Agriculture should be headed by an experienced individual who has spent a lifetime in agriculture. Similarly, the Ministry of Industry should not be given to someone who has never even invented a gadget. This ministry should be led by someone who has invented several things in their career.

Immigrants should also be involved in the decision-making processes concerning the economy of their home country. Immigrants with experience, businesses, and ideas are very valuable tools to improve the well-being of a country. They need to be given the opportunity and sometimes the priority to help and be part of the progress of their homeland.

All citizens should be involved in the decision-making process of any project. Among these citizens are millions of educated, smart individuals with experience and vision. Often, the number of intelligent people among citizens exceeds the number of smart people in any government. I don't understand why some governments think they know better than their citizens and know what's good and bad for them. Money, status, and positions don't necessarily make good presidents and ministers. An official or even an ordinary person with a job, a house, and a car, presumably, has no need to steal or take bribes. Stealing and accepting bribes should be vigorously combated and made a significant shame in society. Other bad manners and substances should be banned and fought against to the maximum to ensure the safety and well-being of children, men, and women. Justice is an essential tool for creating a safe and developed society.

In a perfect society, all jails should be converted into hospitals, and every military barracks should be turned into universities. It is a national decision and priority to transform a society into a perfect one.

Factors of Production

If a country possesses all four factors of production, then it has no excuse not to develop or remain poor. The factors of production are present in almost every country; therefore, each country should work hard to utilize them and economically take off. In addition to land and labor, there is capital. Economists divide capital into two categories: physical capital, which includes money and machines, and mental capital, which encompasses smart people, engineers, scientists, entrepreneurs, and people with ideas. I believe every developing country has an abundant number of these specialists.

Land refers to the multiple natural resources a country possesses to produce goods and services. I assume that most developed countries have these resources. Some countries even have gold and diamonds that could be used to purchase necessary machines, tools, and technology to make the production of goods and services very possible. Instead of using the income from these expensive resources to buy food, medicines, and clothes, these countries can flip the equation and use those revenues to launch a big economy.

Labor refers to the number of people willing to work to produce goods and services. It is well-known these days that developing countries have a huge population of young people who can drive the economy to a very high standard. These young people are just waiting for their governments to gather every resource to launch a robust industry that would improve their lives.

Physical capital refers to the money invested in producing goods and services. Some of this funding could come from the national treasury when designing the national budget, or banks could sponsor these projects. If these are not options, immigrants from these countries could participate in their homeland's economy. Immigrants can establish an organization to collect donations to purchase the necessary machinery needed to produce goods and services. Immigrants often care deeply about their homeland and the well-being of their compatriots. Sometimes, it is a national duty to help if there is a way. At the very least, a person can tell their children that they participated in the development of their country. Moreover, this is an excellent way to teach our children that loving one's country and people is a commendable quality. This is how we build responsible and caring citizens.

Mental capital refers to the abundant number of intelligent people in a particular country. I say this because thousands of students graduate from universities in many different and challenging specialties in every single developing country.

Some of these students are among the brightest in the world. Many of them have graduated from the best universities globally. I myself graduated from an American university and saw firsthand those who graduated with honors; most of them were from developing countries, and I was one of them.

In addition to these individuals, there are thousands, if not millions, of experienced people who can elevate their country to a very high level.

How to Utilize These Factors Efficiently

Among the best ways to efficiently utilize these factors is to:

- Create a national committee to oversee the industry.

- Divide the country into regions and establish a committee in every region. Call for conventions to study how to initiate the new industry.

- Discuss the country's priorities at these conventions. Form tech clubs in every city to foster more ingenuity.

The national committee should first discuss the country's priorities, formulate a plan, and focus on what to produce when to produce it, and for whom to produce it. The committee will be responsible for ensuring that everything functions perfectly. It is prudent to divide the country into regions with subcommittees. Each local committee should strive to gather funds, even through donations if necessary, to open factories and hire engineers and specialists to launch new factories or plants. If a region performs well, other regions should seek advice from it, but if a region is performing poorly, the results will be evident, and it will be clear who is to blame.

The federal government should run contests between states to see who is working hard and progressing. It should reward every committee for hard work and moving the industry in the right direction. From time to time, these committees should hold conventions to discuss achievements, how to improve production and marketing, and look for more ways to save money and time.

More conventions should be held in every field, including agriculture, industry, inventions, medicine, car making, education, tourism, transportation, banking, and computers. Conventions allow the country to assess its direction. They also enable companies to see where they stand in comparison to global companies, and what improvements are needed in their work, goods, and services, as well as setting future goals. Conventions help maintain focus in every field and achieve goals in a very short period, saving time and resources. In the United States, conventions are held weekly, particularly in cities like Orlando, California, and Philadelphia, which host the largest convention centers. Professionals from every sector across the country come to these conventions to discuss new inventions, new business methods, new production techniques, and how to strive to be the best in every aspect.

Priorities and Trivialities

The first priority for a developing country is to be independent in terms of food production. It is crucial for a country to produce its own food; otherwise, it is unreasonable for it to claim independence while relying on food imports. Food production is manageable to cultivate, distribute, and deliver to citizens. Today, many developing countries rely more on imports than on their own production. Fertile lands should be fully utilized to produce as much as possible to feed the nation. The government should clear any unusable lands and convert them into fertile soil. Each farm should employ the right machines, pesticides, and techniques to ensure the proper quantity and quality of fruits and vegetables are produced. The government should establish a solid transportation network to ensure timely delivery of crops to the right locations. The entire industry operates like a chain; if one link breaks, do not expect favorable outcomes. Governments should guide farmers on what to produce, how to produce it, and for whom.

Large supplies of water are essential for agriculture. Developing countries located by the sea or an ocean have a significant advantage—they possess this "liquid gold." Any country with some funds can convert saltwater from the sea or ocean into drinkable water, which is vital for robust agricultural infrastructure.

Greenhouses today use less water than traditional open farming spaces.

The second priority for a developing country to be considered an independent state is to produce its own medicines. With today's technology and the large number of scientists, doctors, and pharmacists, each developing country should be able to produce its own medicines without needing imports. A country that has ample water, produces its own food and medicines, and does not depend on developed countries for these critical resources, can truly rely on itself to move forward.

To provide large quantities of water, food, and medicines, a developing country can create thousands of jobs, making this process feasible. When the quality and production reach high levels, the country can export the surplus of fruits, vegetables, and medicines to other countries for additional revenue.

Competition and Fear

Competition and fear are powerful motivators for development. For instance, if it were not for the Cold War, the US and Russia might not have achieved their current levels of technology, especially in the field of armament. In the 1980s, it was believed that the Soviet Union was ahead of the US by 20 years in space technology. The Soviet Union's achievement in orbiting the Earth was driven by competition. Similarly, the US managed to launch a spaceship that reached the moon due to competition with the Soviet Union. Therefore, competition is a beneficial means to improve almost anything in life.

Fear is also a significant factor in development. For example, Israel, due to fear of its neighbors, has achieved a very high level of development, especially in the fields of arms, telecommunications, and espionage. Similarly, South Korea, because of fear of its neighbor North Korea, has attained a high level of development and sophisticated technology. Today, South Korea ranks as the 13th largest economy in the world.

Developing countries could use the notions of competition and fear to advance to a very high level for economic and military security.

Developing countries can divide the nation into industrialized zones to create competition, monitor the quality and quantity of goods and services, and hold every factory's president accountable. In other words, the government will provide the means of production for every zone, select the right people to run these factories, and set clear expectations for them after thorough studies. These factories must then compete with other zones to produce the best goods and services and sell their products in both local and international markets. A committee would oversee the quality and quantity of these products.

Good presidents should be rewarded for their competition, hard work, and innovation, but failed presidents need to be let go.

The fear of losing his job will motivate a factory president to do whatever it takes to succeed. Unfortunately, the tradition of keeping the same presidents in charge of underperforming factories still exists in developing countries. Additionally, the lack of designated industrial zones results in a lack of inspiration, motivation, or competition to improve. Moreover, it's challenging to assess the quantity and quality of goods and services when there is no competition and nothing to compare them to.

Launching an Economic Revolution would require the following:

National decision-making.

Get the right people in the right place.

Set up a new political system.

Set up a new economic system. Establish plans.

Choose a role model country to emulate.

Ensure freedom of speech for citizens, especially journalists.

Promote quality education.

Eliminate bureaucracy.

Collaborate with everyone.

Organize forums and conventions.

Start with priorities such as food and medicine.

Establish rights to protect citizens' money in banks.

Involve every citizen in every project.

List of Goals to Achieve:

Achieve independence in food and medicine.

Develop a modern industry.

Develop successful agriculture.

Raise the quality of the education system.

Improve the quality of life for citizens.

Manufacture your own military needs.

Maintain a strong military.

Advance in all fields of technology.

Cultivate strong diplomacy.

Excel in all sectors.

Enable local companies to manufacture all needed goods.

Construct a new political structure.

Build a strong government.

Create a competitive economy.

Establish a new political system based on technocracy.

Eliminate bureaucratic challenges.

Guarantee freedom of the press.

Patriotism and National Pride

People and governments should work together to strengthen their country in every possible sector. Nothing is impossible in this world; it is a matter of acknowledging defeat, refuting the circumstances, and then rising and fighting for what's beneficial for the nation's future. There is nothing to lose, especially if a nation is experiencing severe social, economic, health, and educational challenges.

Governments should rally their citizens behind them and raise a sense of patriotism and national pride to overcome poverty or any difficult times, rebuild their countries, and forge a better future for themselves and future generations.

Citizens should assume responsibility towards their country, not just their government because ultimately, it is a duty they owe to their grandchildren, who may one day ask, "Why didn't you do something about it?" As Mahatma Gandhi said, citizens should be the change they want to see in the world.

Developing countries must realize that no one will come to their aid; it's a harsh world, and survival now favors the strongest, not just the fittest. Citizens must also understand that waiting for their government to act is often futile. Sometimes governments lack the money the tools, or both; therefore, people need to rely on themselves, as hard work will eventually bear fruit.

Educating people is where governments need to invest. Although costly, it pays off in the long run. Japan's success is largely due to its focus on education and discipline. Governments should allow only young, educated, and patriotic individuals to lead. As the saying goes, "Someone who has nothing can't give anything." They need to pave the way for the youth because they carry the love for their country and their people. Once a nation is united under one flag, one country, and one leadership, it can make a significant difference in society. Hostile tribes, races, aborigines, and immigrants should make peace and unite to lead the country out of darkness. History shows that petty conflicts have never worked in any country at any time; they only drag countries deeper into poverty and misery. All citizens should learn from the world around them that every conflict breeds more conflict. The only thing that can bring all people together is their country, its destiny, and the fate of future generations. Everyone has children, and everyone should be conscientious about what they will do to make the country a better place for them to live in. It is the responsibility of all citizens to set aside personal pride and ego and embrace national pride to launch an economic revolution strong enough to elevate the standard of living for all communities.

To achieve this, governments must educate their people through commercials, propaganda, billboards, schools, and every available means of communication to instill a national spirit that motivates them to rise and build their countries. We should be ashamed not to work hard and let other nations lead the world; we should be leaders as well; enough of being followers all the time. There is no difference between people in the North and people in the South except in their work ethic. Working hard should not be an option; it should be a national mandate to lift people out of poverty, misery, and the social problems that have plagued every aspect of our lives.

Governments should also invest time and money in educating citizens about scientists and leaders who have achieved the impossible so they can take them as role models with the goal of fixing everything that is not functioning properly. Cities and streets should also be named after world scientists, inventors, leaders, and philosophers who led their societies toward success and development.

Choose a Role Model Country and Follow It

If a developing country finds it complicated to launch an economy, all it needs to do is choose a developed country that it believes is performing well and follow its steps closely. There are multiple developed countries around the world, and each one approaches things in its own way. Remember that no two economies are identical; each is shaped by its own geography, resources, laws, culture, and history.

Some countries are lucky to be situated near oceans, seas, or rivers, which offer better locations than landlocked countries. Some countries possess almost all the resources necessary for production, while others have few or almost none, but either way, there are always steps that can be taken to make progress.

Some countries have restrictive laws that hinder national progress. For example, in some countries, only the government can produce goods and services, and in others, only the government can import or export items. Some countries prohibit citizens from importing cars from overseas. Some don't allow farmers to sell their products directly to foreign countries; sales must go through the government. In any case, the lack of freedom in conducting business prevents high economic performance.

Culture has been influencing our way of life since childhood. Each nation practices commerce differently; sometimes, it works, and sometimes it hinders the economy. For instance, Chinese and Japanese societies have a strong work ethic rooted in their culture, a major element that has revitalized their economies. In contrast, in some developing countries, instead of working hard, many people spend hours in cafes playing chess because it is part of their culture. Other cultural aspects that positively impact the Japanese and Chinese economies include devotion, discipline, unity, and humility. Japanese culture, for example, highly values hard work and long hours. Other positive cultural elements in Japan include high educational standards and religious practices. Shintoism, for instance, requires people to be extremely clean to be considered pure and devout.

History can also hinder economic progress. Hundreds of years of colonialism, servitude, slavery, and poor education continue to affect the ways developing countries operate. A long history of financial crises, corruption, and economic mismanagement by numerous officials has been a major obstacle to progress.

However, a country serious about launching its economy should not dwell on these negative factors but should instead look to countries that have achieved great economic success. The US, Japan, Germany, Finland, China, and even Turkey are good role models. The leaders, as mentioned in several chapters, need to make decisive choices about establishing a robust economy to elevate their country and its people to a higher standard. Through national staff at embassies, as mentioned in a previous chapter, in developed countries, they could study how these nations manage their economies. In other words, gather data, study how these countries produce crops, goods, and services, analyze successful government forms, understand banking operations, and examine educational systems. They could also emulate not only the methods but also the speed and quality with which highways, bridges, and skyscrapers are built.

In 1871, during the Meiji Restoration in Japan—a major revolution that brought about a new democratic, social, and political system leading to significant economic reforms and growth—the country adopted a similar approach and formed the Iwakura Mission. The government sent over 100 top government officials, scholars, and brilliant students, primarily to the US, France, Germany, Belgium, Switzerland, Britain, and Russia. The missionaries examined, noted, and meticulously recorded all aspects of American and European societies, from agriculture to industry, education, commerce, and even politics. Right after the expedition, Japan realized that it was necessary to implement new policies deliberately to enrich the country through modernization and industrialization.

Similar expeditions could be undertaken today by developing countries to replicate past successes. It is merely a matter of goodwill and good intentions— "Where there is a will, there is a way," as the saying goes.

Zoning

Zoning, as mentioned in previous chapters, is a strategic approach to keep industries, agriculture, and production well-structured, managed, and supervised. A country could be divided into four parts or zones, each overseen by committees.

For instance, there could be a committee for car production, a committee for agricultural production, and a committee for other large-scale productions.

To elaborate, each region should have a certain number of farms, firms, factories, and plants. All these units should ideally belong to the government, which, in my belief, cares more about its citizens and national interests compared to big corporations and private owners, who may care less. Each industry should then be supervised by a committee whose task is to ensure that every unit has the money and tools to produce goods and services as efficiently as possible. The committee is also responsible for overseeing production in each sector and for appointing the right person to lead each industry. This leader will be rewarded for excellent performance. Conversely, performing poorly will cost this director their job, as there is no more time to waste, especially in developing countries where time is of the essence. This policy will keep everyone focused and motivated to do a better job.

The advantage of zoning also includes being able to see which region benefits the country and which does not. In some cases, one or two states might carry the burden for the rest of the country, and since production is ongoing, the other plants and factories may care less. By zoning a country, each region will compete to be the best and will be recognized and rewarded consistently.

Competition—another factor of modernization—between regions will lead to excellence and progress. The chances of failure are very slim because everyone is accountable, and every worker is fulfilling their duties. If things go wrong in any sector, the committees are there to intervene, correct any wrongdoing, and get the unit back on track. Monitoring and supervising every step of each sector's performance is crucial to addressing any production that is sluggish and costs the government too much money and stress.

It would be a great idea not to pay managers and employees excessive amounts, but rather a decent salary with benefits and quarterly bonuses. Bonuses are an effective way to motivate both workers and managers. In other words, if you give a regular employee a fixed salary, they might not care about the output since they are getting paid that specific income anyway. However, once they know that there is a bonus for high output, they will work harder to achieve it. American companies and corporations use this technique to motivate employees to perform better, and trust me, it works.

Above all, there should be a national committee that works directly with the zones' committees and reports everything to the appropriate seniors or cabinet members. All the information and statistics from all sectors would eventually be provided to the president to assess the country's status.

In the US, there is an economic committee at the White House that works directly with the president; its job is to oversee the economy and the markets. Every morning, alongside the political briefing, an economic briefing is reported to the president with data regarding consumption, imports, and exports of necessary resources that are needed to keep the economy moving in the right direction. The committee also informs him of any potential resource shortages, which countries have those resources, the nature of the relations the US has with those countries, and how to acquire those resources from them. Through this procedure, the president is always aware of almost everything that goes on in the country; a brilliant idea that helps keep everything in order.

Construction

Construction is the most efficient way to create jobs consistently. The construction of thousands of buildings, thousands of miles of roads to be built, paved, maintained, and millions of miles of highways to be laid will require millions of workers to be completed properly and on time. It is indeed a great way to provide jobs as long as the government has a plan to keep construction progressing at the same rate as population growth. For instance, constructing highways will require thousands of workers for tasks ranging from clearing lands to installing highway lights. The same applies to other construction projects such as airports, hospitals, administrative buildings, jails, barracks, offices, schools, etc. By undertaking all these works, the government of any country should be in a great condition.

Unfortunately, in some developing countries, governments complain that their people are lazy and want everything handed to them. Governments tend to make citizens feel that they are the cause of their own demise, according to Noam Chomsky. At the same time, when you ask the people if that is true, they tell you there are no jobs in any sector and there are no factories to begin with. So, it is a mutual accusation that needs to be addressed. Anyway, a government of any country has to educate its people about everything it does for the country and its citizens. A government should educate its people about the purpose of construction, agriculture, education, and everything else it intends to do. As discussed in previous chapters, citizens should be involved in the decision-making of any major project that takes place in their country. Citizens don't like unnecessary projects because they suspect the purpose behind them is to embezzle funds. The government also has the obligation to motivate citizens to take these jobs by offering them good salaries. Some governments purposely bring in foreign companies and workers, leaving their own people without jobs. The excuse is that those foreign workers work better and faster, and it's unclear if cheaper.

Most of the projects rendered by foreign companies are extremely expensive. Thus, it is in the self-interest of both the government and citizens to work together to accomplish any project. Bringing foreign companies and workers is never good for the economy. Not only do they charge a lot of money, but they also tend to monopolize more projects, leaving the local people without jobs, and even begin to intervene in the politics of that particular country. They buy land, failing companies, shares, houses, and eventually begin to influence government decisions.

Once a government educates its citizens about the benefits of working in construction, such as helping the economy, creating jobs, gaining experience, and displacing foreign companies so they don't get involved in the country's politics, it should become a matter of national pride to accomplish everything locally.

Governments can also circumvent the need for foreign companies by hiring only engineers, architects, and specialists who have performed marvelously worldwide. The process involves searching for successful projects and identifying who was behind them. The government can then make attractive offers to these engineers and architects, which they are unlikely to refuse. No matter how much money these professionals are paid, it will never equate to the cost of employing completely foreign companies with their workers. Once these engineers and architects arrive in the country, the government should support these projects with local engineers, architects, and thousands of workers. All of these local workers need to pay close attention to everything those foreign engineers and architects do so they can learn from their talents, experience, and methods. This valuable exposure will provide local workers with the opportunity to learn how to perform exceptional work, just like their foreign counterparts.

Local workers must understand that this learning is necessary for the survival of their country, citizens, and future generations. It should be part of the education and upbringing instilled in every successful and responsible nation.

Even if the country runs out of construction projects, which I doubt, governments can still create jobs to boost the economy by demolishing and rebuilding cities, towns, and buildings one by one. Spain underwent a similar process during its Great Recession from 2008 to 2014.

Even prisoners can participate in the economy; tasks such as cleaning streets, painting, and construction can be undertaken by prisoners who have only a few months left to serve. This approach, used in the US, helps convicts acquire a skill so they can find employment upon release instead of returning to crime. Cities provide an opportunity for convicts to learn something and become good citizens.

By using just a few foreign engineers and local workers, the government will save a lot of money. Meanwhile, local workers will gain significant experience from these foreign engineers and can use this knowledge for future projects without needing to call on foreign experts. When foreign companies approached China to open up for commerce and development, China said, "We will provide everything from land, cheap labor, and tax incentives to marketing; however, you don't just make goods for us, we want you to teach us how to make them." Essentially, China was seeking the technology behind the products, knowing that once they learned how to manufacture these goods, they could do it independently. Now, look at China—almost the top economy with the best technology in the world. In addition, China, today, has the largest amount of cash in the world. It is said that for every Dollar that circulates in the US, 0.60 cents belong to Chinese banks.

Today, developing countries should have the upper hand because of all the resources they possess. They could even demand from foreign countries every existing technology, including how to manufacture a Bugatti or a Concorde.

Unfortunately, there are still barriers that maintain the status quo and prevent citizens in developing countries from advancing.

Vehicle Production

If a country decides to start vehicle production, the vision should be straightforward and uncomplicated. For instance, the country might aim to produce four types of cars, four types of SUVs, four types of pickup trucks, four types of commercial trucks, and four types of buses. Recall that we divided the country into zones, right? All the auto assemblies could be divided among these regions or zones to create thousands of jobs, thus distributing employment evenly across the country. Also, remember that we mentioned each car requires about 30,000 pieces to be ready for sale. Imagine how many factories could be built to manufacture all these pieces, and consider the number of jobs that would be created. Imagine the number of pieces needed to produce thousands, if not millions, of autos. It's just a matter of taking the right steps, and everything will be set on track.

I also mentioned in the zoning section that each committee must ensure that each industry succeeds. By thriving in the auto industry, the country will be able to supply the local markets with all types of cars, SUVs, trucks, etc. This will enable each family to fulfill its dream of owning a vehicle. More cars mean more roads, more highways, more bridges, more drivers, more gas stations, and more production of everything a car and a gas station need.

By producing more local autos and spare parts, the country will reduce its dependence on the North. The country will purchase only the items that cannot be produced locally. More autos mean the country will be able to compete in the global auto industry; nice cars with attractive features and competitive prices can allow the country to export them to other parts of the world. More exports also mean more money coming into the country. As a result, people will have jobs and lead better lives.

If a country acquires this type of technology, it will then be positioned to manufacture trains, boats, and even ships and airplanes. The country also needs a robust transportation infrastructure to facilitate the movement of merchandise and people efficiently. The large volumes of agricultural and industrial goods require a fast and efficient transportation system so these products can reach the markets quickly. Some products are perishable, and others need timely delivery due to contractual obligations and needs.

Agriculture

Though I discussed agriculture in a previous chapter, here I will be more specific. To establish a strong and successful agriculture, the country must first be divided into zones based on the type of production. Each zone will specialize in producing the crops best suited to that area. To achieve this, the government needs to consult with farmers in those zones to determine which crops will thrive in their region.

Fertile lands must be reserved exclusively for agricultural activities. This can be enforced through laws passed by the Ministry of Agriculture or by Parliament. Fertile lands are the lungs of any country. Private owners may use their fertile lands for crop production, but they must not leave them unused. If lands are not utilized, the government has the right to take over due to national interest. Private owners should not be allowed to sell these lands for any purpose other than crop production. Today, in developing countries, because land is so valuable, owners are selling their fertile lands to private companies and corporations and even to individuals for various projects. For them, instead of dealing with the challenges of farming—such as tilling, watering, and maintaining the land to make some money—it's easier to sell the land and make millions of dollars quickly and effortlessly.

If any farmer decides to sell his lands, the government should be the only entity allowed to purchase those lands since they are vital for the nation's survival.

Currently, in many developing countries, concrete is encroaching upon a lot of fertile lands.

Secondly, each region will be supervised by a committee to ensure that farmers have the necessary tools and pesticides to produce sufficient and appropriate crops. Left to their own devices, farmers might produce whatever they want, not what consumers need. Sometimes, farmers opt to grow expensive fruits and vegetables because they seek quick profits. Some farmers control the production, distribution, and storage of certain items to keep prices high, thus maximizing their profits. It is imperative to monitor the agricultural sector constantly because, nowadays, farmers are manipulating the markets for their benefit.

From this point, I suggest that the government should take ownership of all fertile lands in the country. The government is more concerned about the well-being of its citizens than the private sector. I know what you might be thinking—that this approach could lead to governmental dictatorship. However, we'd rather live under an economic dictatorship that cares about the public good than at the mercy of ruthless corporations focused solely on maximizing their profits for minimal effort.

I have to say that in developing countries, there is no coordination between farmers and the government; the government expects farmers to produce but never meets with them to discuss their concerns, their needs, or the best ways to increase production to supply the market with all types of fruits and vegetables. In other words, every farmer produces whatever he feels like, or is able to, which is why production is always weak and market supplies are insufficient.

Second, the government should be involved in agriculture from planting to when the products reach the markets. The government should also provide farmers with pesticides, tractors, trucks, and refrigerators—all the necessary tools to facilitate production. Farmers are crucial to the well-being of a nation. We need farmers more than we need doctors. We may need a doctor occasionally, but we need a farmer every day we go to the supermarket. If the government is heavily involved in other sectors, why doesn't it engage as intensely in agriculture?

As I mentioned in the Fall of Socialism chapter, the government should clear the land, divide it into parcels, provide all the necessary tools, and distribute these lands to those willing to work seriously. The government also needs to appoint someone in charge and hold him accountable while also providing a very good salary to ensure he performs well; otherwise, his failure will cost him his job. This is a good way to motivate every manager!

Third, the government must build a robust transportation network to move all merchandise from farms to markets. By mobilizing everyone and implementing these steps, the government is creating thousands of jobs. Agriculture should be nurtured carefully from the farm all the way to the consumer. By taking these steps, the government will ensure abundant production of all types of fruits and vegetables, as well as reasonable prices for consumers. Speculation has no place when the government closely monitors this process.

The government also has to keep an eye on the fishing industry. Prices of fish in developing countries are extremely high, similar to red and white meats. Some fishermen now catch only a little to keep prices high. In this case, the government must intervene and turn things around. Private farmers, fishermen, and corporations have become ruthless and do not care about consumers or their purchasing power. When private sectors control the production and sale of all necessities, consumers often direct their anger at the government, believing it is responsible for high prices and their misery. Therefore, it is in the government's self-interest to get involved in the production of crops, fish, and even dairy products to ensure that consumers can afford them. Expensive food leads to more hungry people, and more hungry people mean more angry people. These individuals will turn to the government for benefits and help, which can cost the government millions of dollars. If the government has money, it can provide direct assistance or help people buy groceries, but if it lacks funds, it may either print more money, create inflation, or borrow from other countries, adding to its foreign debts. Either solution is damaging to the country.

Again, for public security, the government should not allow the private sector to control every product or market. Ultimately, the private sector is removed from the challenges the government faces. The government might even face an uprising due to hunger or high prices. Sometimes, these uprisings can escalate, and many lives could be lost. In contrast, the government deals with the chaos; private owners and the wealthy watch from the sidelines. There is a saying, "Revolutions are planned by educated people, executed by poor people, and benefited from by rich people." Surprisingly, after each revolution, the government promises reforms, and guess what? Each time there are reforms, only the rich or the private sector benefit.

Moreover, according to the world-renowned sociologist Ibn Khaldun, "hunger can lead people to transgression"; in simple terms, when people become hungry, they will do anything to obtain food. They can become depressed or violent, turn to drugs or prostitution, or resort to stealing. Each of these outcomes will cost the government millions of dollars, so it is better to anticipate all of this. As the saying goes, "To govern means to predict."

Fourth, farmers should strive to produce more than enough food for consumers. It should be a matter of national pride to produce surplus food for the people. An increased supply means lower prices, which in turn helps maintain the value of the currency. An ample food supply can help the government trade the excess for other necessary items with other countries. Additionally, a surplus can be stored in case of any disaster or shortage.

Fifth, each zone will compete with others to produce more and become the leader. Each zone and the people in charge should be rewarded for their efforts to make agriculture a success. When one region feeds the entire country, the rest of the regions might stop working as hard since another carries the burden.

Typically, in scenarios like this, one region compensates for the failures of others. Thus, having designated zones will make it easier to pinpoint problems and fix any sector of agriculture effectively.

It is highly recommended to use machines extensively to achieve a large output of crops. A surplus of crops is always beneficial for bartering.

The extensive use of machinery can also be employed to clear millions of acres of land for producing all types of fruits and vegetables, as well as creating grazing lands for cattle. Grazing lands are essential for a country's survival. For instance, Ethiopia has achieved a high number of cattle, estimated at 60 million heads and about 70 million cows—a staggering number for a developing country.

By having millions of cows, a significant number of dairy farms will emerge. Dairy farming dates back to the seventh millennium BC, during the Neolithic era. These farms will be capable of producing not only enough milk, butter, and cheese for local consumption but also a surplus for security reasons and for bartering. More dairy products in a country means more workers are needed, which would lead to lower prices; lower prices mean happy consumers. In the US, there are over 60,000 dairy farms; that's a lot of farms producing a lot of milk, cheese, and butter. As a result, milk is available at any time of the day. In 2022, the US produced 222 billion pounds of dairy products; this is a valuable lesson to learn from the US experience on how to manage this industry. This success is not magic; it's about replicating their methods.

Fish farming is essential in countries where fishermen are not providing sufficient quantities to meet market demand; therefore, adopting this effective technique is necessary. Since red and white meats are expensive and many consumers in developing countries cannot afford them, fish farming can be a viable alternative for protein. It's a straightforward process that requires serious decision-making, dedication, and extra care.

A professor from Florida International University was invited to Haiti to conduct a case study aimed at improving the local economy of a specific area. The professor observed that there was not enough red and white meat available for all the residents, and the prices were prohibitively high. He suggested that the locals find an alternative source of protein and allow the livestock to breed for some time.

Since sheep and cows give birth only once a year, he recommended switching to rabbits, which breed three to four times a year and can produce up to twelve litters each time. Studies show that rabbit meat is a good source of protein, contains zero carbohydrates, and is very low in cholesterol, making it ideal for people who monitor their cholesterol and fat levels. By adopting this strategy, a country could allow its livestock to breed peacefully, and prices would automatically decrease as the supply increased.

By implementing all these techniques, a country can produce enough food, red and white meats, and fish not only to meet its own demands but also to sell surplus to other countries. It is always beneficial to think big and aim high.

Tourism

Tourism is a natural revenue generator for many countries. Some countries are fortunate to possess multiple exotic natural sites, while others boast romantic locations that attract visitors. However, it's important to recognize that these sites didn't just appear; they were developed by insightful individuals for various reasons. Today, countries such as France, Spain, Italy, and the UK are generating billions of dollars in revenue from tourism. Achieving this is not magic or particularly difficult; it simply requires visionary planning. Before discussing strategies to build this economy, let's review some landmarks and sites and the significant revenue they generate for their countries. For example, France is the most visited country in the world, attracting over 100 million tourists from all over the globe thanks to its rich history and iconic landmarks. According to Campus France, in 2022, France generated approximately 58 billion Euros in tourism revenue. This staggering amount should motivate citizens in developing countries to engage in building a similar economy.

According to Barron, Spain is the world's second most popular tourist destination after France. In 2022, Spain attracted over 70 million tourists, predominantly from Germany, the UK, and France, amassing a record $159 billion in revenue. Italy recorded $190 billion, and the UK surpassed $26 billion.

Even Turkey, as reported by Trading Economics, generated about $13 billion from tourism in 2023. Even taking the smallest revenue figure from tourism in Turkey as an example, it could potentially finance an industrial revolution in any developing country.

Earning money from tourism is relatively straightforward. It does not require geniuses or heavy equipment and technology; it simply involves creating a few landmarks that become the talk of the town. It is in the best interest of developing countries to focus on building a portion of their economy based on tourism. In fact, for some countries with limited resources, tourism may be the only viable solution to build their economy. The initial investment required is not substantial, but the returns can be significant and continuous.

How to Build a Tourism Infrastructure

To begin, a country must establish zero tolerance for littering. The environment should be impeccably clean. Governments should educate their citizens about the benefits of clean streets and readiness to embrace tourism as a sign of development and a source of income. For example, Japan is considered one of the cleanest countries in the world, and developing countries could emulate its practices.

Japanese cities are not only clean because the citizens are committed to maintaining a clean environment but also because Shintoism teaches that cleanliness is essential to religious purity.

Secondly, the country should engage people with creative ideas, architects, and artists to collaborate on designing thrilling landmarks. Each city should be encouraged to contribute at least a dozen unique and exciting landmarks. Cities could also hold competitions to determine who can create the most beautiful landmark that is both easy and economical to construct.

Sculptors could play a significant role in erecting statues and monuments and even creating another Mount Rushmore with a different vision and personality. Each city should have at least one museum where it can display every precious piece of art to make that museum an icon. Schools and colleges should also run competitions for the best artwork that deserves to be showcased in museums. It is worth mentioning that the Louvre Museum in Paris, France, generates over 100 million Euros annually and that the Mona Lisa alone is valued at $1 billion—enough to build roughly 100 factories.

Dozens of gardens with fountains, lakes, and thousands of amazing flowers and roses are essential if we aim to elevate tourism. It is possible and achievable; we just need the will to be the best.

Having seashores is a tremendous asset for a developing country. It is a blessing and a powerful tool to attract tourists from all over the world. All that is needed is a great plan and great people to make it happen. Every city by the shore should work on creating a dozen exotic resorts, hotels, and beaches. It's not magic; a country could replicate some of the finest resorts, hotels, and beaches in the world. All that is needed is to add a unique twist and a different note to every place.

To make these resorts attractive and popular, the government must invest in marketing and train people to promote tourism. The country needs to withstand a little economic strain initially to attract tourists and introduce them to this new experience. In other words, prices should not compete with those in Europe, for instance. It is crucial to recognize that when tourists realize that visiting these resorts costs less than other destinations, they will undoubtedly opt for the more economical choice.

The government also has the duty to provide a fleet of airlines with excellent service and affordable tickets to bring in tourists. Airports should be immaculate as well. Employees also have the duty to deliver perfect service to tourists and make them feel special so they will enjoy this new experience and not hesitate to return with friends and colleagues. By ensuring safety, good accommodation, excellent service, delicious food, and a clean environment, the number of tourists will increase each year.

Having a lot of tourists should be good news for leaders and the country because several beneficial outcomes will result. First, the country will establish a new economic infrastructure that will last for a long time and serve future generations. Second, tourists will bring more currency into the country, just as they do in France, Spain, and Italy. The resorts, new amenities, museums, and local stores will heavily sell their products, services, and souvenirs to tourists. Additionally, wealthy tourists may also become interested in investing in the country. Third, an important element in the economy of any country, is that the multiple resorts and amenities will need to hire thousands of employees to make this magical experience smooth and possible. Fourth, more food and supplies will be sold to the resorts. Remember, every little thing that you add to make tourism successful also creates jobs along the way.

Recycling

Many developing countries do not recycle their trash for various reasons. In fact, 70% of trash could be recycled and used again. Recycling is among the key ingredients for launching a new economic revolution, if we may say so. In addition to fixing the most important elements, such as education, industry, and agriculture, recycling could be one of those pivotal elements for several reasons. Recycling saves money, resources, and time, and most importantly, it raises awareness about the future of humans and our Planet Earth.

Today, Germany is a leader in recycling and waste management. The success of this major leap is due to two factors: high public awareness of the benefits of recycling and strong government policies. Germany has adopted an effective recycling system that allows it to recycle 60% of its daily trash, making it number one in the world. A new culture has emerged in Germany concerning saving the planet by recycling.

Germany has developed a system to encourage people to participate in recycling. A person has to pay a deposit for a can or a bottle, usually about 25 cents. Once the cans and bottles are returned to special machines in supermarkets, the person gets their deposit back. This system is rigorous and ingenious at the same time, but it's worth it to protect our Planet Earth.

Recycling allows a country to reduce the depletion of its resources, import fewer goods from other countries—which saves a lot of money—and creates a culture of responsibility towards the country and Mother Earth. Plastic, paper, cans, and glass can be recycled over and over, and each time they are reused, the country saves significant funds. This culture of recycling raises public awareness about the environment and encourages all citizens to be responsible towards their country and the planet.

Developed countries use heat from burning waste, such as paper, plastic, products made from wood, yard waste, and even livestock manure, to produce steam in a boiler which is used to power electric generator turbines to produce electricity and to heat buildings. In 2021, the US used 64 power plants to produce 13.6 billion kilowatts of electricity. It is said that 1200 tons of trash can supply 4000 homes with power in the US.

Recycling used water is another straightforward process that can help any country remain clean, produce more crops, import fewer fruits and vegetables, and ultimately save a lot of money. With water becoming increasingly scarce, some scientists expect wars to break out between nations over water resources.

Consequently, nations are rapidly turning to purifying their used water or using desalination to provide more water for drinking, as well as for watering crops and gardens. In Israel, for example, what was once a distressing water shortage has now become a surplus. Today, Israel employs a combination of recycling, conservation, and desalination to meet its water needs. According to statistics, Israel now has more water than it needs.

Saudi Arabia is another example of a country that is desalinating water from the Red Sea and the Arabian Gulf. The country now operates more than 27 desalination plants, providing half of its drinking water, and is considered the world's largest producer of desalinated water.

Developing countries that are fortunate enough to border seas or oceans can do the same. It is a straightforward process; it just requires some investment and the will to implement it, and it is certainly worth it. Ample water supplies mean that the country can plant a lot of crops, have water for survival, and keep all the streets clean.

Technology and Jobs

Technology has played a significant role in improving societies, boosting economies, and creating millions of jobs. At the beginning of the 20th century, new inventions such as cars, telephones, airplanes, washing machines, elevators, and refrigerators created thousands, if not millions, of jobs worldwide. This led to a major shift in the lifestyle of millions of people. Societies transitioned from being predominantly agricultural to administrative and technologically driven, thus pushing the economy in a new and improved direction. Car, telephone, and airplane manufacturing alone employed millions of workers. Citizens began to use technological products at home, at work, and in various facilities. The standard of living improved, and people started to pursue different aspirations.

Governments should encourage consumers to purchase more technological products; the more products they buy, the more jobs are created. Workers can specialize in different sectors, such as manufacturing, repairing, and servicing these technological goods. Ultimately, thousands of jobs will be created, boosting the economy of a country and reducing the number of unemployed. Therefore, developing countries should invest in technology to create jobs and propel their economies forward. To achieve this, governments must take serious steps and make it a priority. By making robust economic decisions, a country will be able to invent and produce goods for both local and external consumption. The goal should not only be to satisfy local markets but also to penetrate foreign markets, leading to increased demand, more investors, and generating more revenue for the country.

The invention of cars has amassed the largest number of workers in industries like the US auto sector. Today, more than 1.7 million Americans are employed by the auto industry. Apple is another major employer, with more than 2 million employees worldwide. In the realm of air travel, Lufthansa employs over 100,000 employees and boasts assets of $46 billion. These are just three examples of the hundreds of inventions from the previous century that have created employment for millions. Thus, alongside construction, technology is the second most effective way to create jobs in any country at any time.

Education and Requirements

Education and job requirements are crucial in the development of a country. Unfortunately, most developing countries do not place the right people in the right positions, leading to widespread complaints about the quality of goods and services provided by these unskilled individuals. Dropouts occupy a large number of key positions in these countries.

For instance, unskilled individuals are detrimental to a country's development. A dropout should not be in charge of critical sectors like the economy or health or even run a daycare. In some developing countries, the requirements for certain jobs, such as teaching or nursing, are stringent. To become a teacher, for example, one must graduate from high school, complete 4 years of college, and pass a national or local exam to qualify for the job. Unfortunately, most states hire only a small number of teachers. On the other hand, to become a mayor or a parliament representative, no educational level or tests are required—an equation that does not make sense. Some of these officials have never attended school. These unskilled mayors cannot effectively support their cities or citizens, and similarly, uneducated representatives cannot adequately represent their constituents or engage in meaningful debates about their well-being.

Ironically, citizens in developing countries point out the inefficiency of these unskilled individuals. Yet, nothing has ever been done to change the rules or the requirements to place the right people in the right positions to lift the country out of its misery. It is a persistent practice to assign unskilled people to sensitive positions despite the fact that these countries suffer in every sector and have for many years.

At this juncture, governments need to change the rules if they wish to improve the well-being of their country and the lives of their citizens. Governments are also urged to motivate educated individuals and those with relevant knowledge and experience to step in, fill these positions, and do what is necessary to advance the interests of the people.

Schools

Schools should give more opportunities to kids to explore, think outside the box, and take part in building their country. There is a saying, "Sometimes you find precious stuff in the river that you can't find in the oceans." Sometimes students have better ideas than their teachers, and sometimes citizens have better ideas than their presidents and cabinet members. For instance, students should be given the freedom to write poems, articles, plays, books, and stories, and they should conduct research on certain topics. They should also be able to paint, design, and create sculptures to decorate their schools, cities, and country. Unleashing students' intelligence can help harness the best in them and shift societal thinking to a higher dimension.

The Minister of Education should consider implementing a double-shift schooling system. The first group of students would attend from early morning until midday and the second group from midday to late afternoon. We could have girls in the morning and boys in the afternoon. Each group would use the same buildings, equipment, and facilities. Four or five hours of effective schooling are sufficient and manageable. Some might worry about kids being in the streets the rest of the day, but the remaining time should be dedicated to homework, research, and sports activities, which are part of the curriculum. This could be managed at home or in libraries where additional help is provided by staff assigned by the school districts for free—a technique used by American colleges and universities. School students should utilize all stadiums and arenas to fulfill their curriculum. Cities spend millions of dollars on stadiums and arenas to watch a local team play once a week; the rest of the week, they remain unused. We could make them beneficial for students as well. Thus, we would not only have smart kids but healthy ones, too.

Finland, which boasts the best education system in the world, only uses 20 hours of teaching per week, equating to 4 hours a day. In 2023, the national Finnish literacy rate was at 100%, compared to 79% in the US. Despite the American government spending billions of dollars on education, over 43 million American adults cannot read or write above a third-grade level (according to literacy statistics). Finland has the highest number of geniuses per capita, according to data from MENSA. Following Finland, Sweden and the UK rank highly in terms of the number of genius individuals.

Schools have become congested in many countries, especially in developing countries, with 40 to 50 students per class. Some students can't use a desk because there aren't enough. The lack of funding has deterred governments from building more schools or even maintaining existing ones. Many schools lack basic amenities like heating, air conditioning, school buses, and cafeterias, and some even lack water.

Implementing a double-shift system could be a brilliant solution. In this setup, the number of students in classes would drop, allowing teachers to focus more effectively on teaching. Classes should be engaging, concise, and straight to the point, fostering more thinking and brainstorming and less writing.

Having fewer students in classes means that the outcomes will be impressive. When the second shift starts in the afternoon, it would have entirely different teachers, principals, and administration. By doing so, the government can create thousands of jobs.

To elevate societies, teachers should be held in extremely high regard, much as doctors are in the United States. This is how teachers are viewed in Japan and Finland, where teachers undoubtedly have a significant impact on a child's life and future. In Japan, teachers are treated with greater respect than in the United States. Children do not address their teachers by their last names but call them "sensei," an honorific title meaning master, which is also used for doctors, authors, and members of parliament. Each morning, before entering the class, Japanese children bow to their teachers—a small gesture that signifies great respect.

Uniforms can provide structure for children. There are several benefits to wearing uniforms: they reduce distractions, enhance study ethics, improve discipline, and save valuable class time. Uniform policies are easier to enforce than a standard dress code, promote equality, remove peer pressure, and reduce bullying. They deter the display of gang colors and symbols and can simplify mornings for both students and parents. The use of uniforms reinforces the idea that school is a serious business.

Professors with PhDs and doctorates should be allowed to teach at various educational levels, not just at colleges and universities. Such professors can elevate the standard of education significantly. I worked with a professor from Florida Atlantic University, USA, who also taught at an elementary school. She enjoyed working with young children and believed that this age was when they could learn the most.

Discipline, coupled with high educational standards, can lead to forming a strong workforce and contribute to a robust modernization process. Acquiring and mastering high technology will advance the country and its citizens. Additionally, teaching other international languages is essential, especially English, which has become the language of international communication. It is the language of science, technology, trade, diplomacy, computers, aviation, and tourism. Proficiency in English can open doors to unlimited research, discoveries, references, books, and laboratories.

Competition Between Universities

Competition among universities can propel a country toward new inventions, directions, and ways of life. Such competition can motivate students to excel. Students will strive to achieve their best, unlocking their greatest potential. Special attention should also be paid to genius students, encouraging them to delve into math, physics, chemistry, inventions, and technology. If each school and university produces one inventor per year, a country could boast at least 1,000 inventors annually. Imagine the impact of 1,000 new inventors each year—the country would burgeon with new technological goods, machines, robots, gadgets, tools, and services.

Cities should actively search for brilliant kids within schools and provide them with the necessary tools and funding to excel and invent. I suggest that at the end of each year, cities should organize competitions to discover who has developed the best inventions. These inventions should be taken seriously and implemented. You never know—another Steve Jobs could be living in your city unnoticed.

Another Bill Gates could be sitting next to you, unknown. Another Thomas Edison could be your neighbor, and you have no idea. Great inventions can elevate a country to a higher standard. Governments in developing countries should take decisive steps to materialize these inventions by building factories, assembly lines, and plants, hiring people, and doing their utmost to turn these inventions into reality. New inventions can open new avenues to enhance citizens' lives and boost the economy of that particular country.

Each state or city should establish tech clubs to discover more genius individuals and uncover their talents. Inventions by these individuals should be taken into serious consideration; their works explored, produced, and marketed globally.

These new pioneers could save an entire nation if given the opportunity to reveal their creativity and ingenuity.

Competition Between Cities

Competition between cities can elevate tourism to a higher level, providing significant revenue for the country. Countries like France, the UK, and Spain, which rely heavily on tourism, ensure that the landscape of each city is

well-maintained. Governments focus on keeping cities clean, safe, and full of amenities. Developing countries should strive to make their cities and neighborhoods clean, safe, and attractive for tourism. Governments can encourage local cities to participate in competitions to determine which city is the cleanest, safest, and most captivating. They should either reward governors and mayors for excellence or hold their jobs accountable for failures.

Clean and safe cities are not only appealing to tourists but also to local citizens. When residents see that their cities are well-maintained, they appreciate their leaders' efforts to enhance their quality of life. A clean and safe environment also indicates that leaders care about their constituents. Ultimately, such cities merit re-electing their governors and mayors for their outstanding governance.

Citizens also play a crucial role in enhancing their cities. They should collaborate with their leaders to improve their living environments. Residents should not rely solely on the city for maintenance; in developed countries, for instance, city workers manage major public areas, but homeowners and renters are responsible for smaller streets and their properties. To promote involvement, governments should educate and motivate citizens about the benefits of maintaining clean and safe cities. Moreover, governments can encourage residents to compete to make their cities the best in the country. To achieve this, governments should employ additional cleaning staff, painters, gardeners, construction and maintenance personnel, and even artists to create murals, sculptures, and fountains. Each city should devise unique ideas to distinguish itself. Icons like the Statue of Liberty, the Taj Mahal, the Eiffel Tower, and the Arc de Triomphe could inspire unique local landmarks. When cities are exemplary, residents feel proud of their lifestyle, boast about their cities, and foster a strong sense of belonging and national pride.

Customer Service and Its Impact on Sales

In order for a country to improve the level and quality of service, it should implement a grading system in nearly every field. Grading teaches people how to be good citizens, professionals, and responsible individuals. It acts as a form of social education. For example, in the US, grading is prevalent across almost all types of businesses and administrations to ensure that each sector meets citizens' expectations.

At American post offices, once a customer completes a transaction, the clerk prints a receipt that includes a telephone number or an online survey about the service provided. This method helps enhance customer service.

Another example is the automotive industry. Two or three days after purchasing a vehicle, a dealership representative will call the customer to ask several questions about their experience and satisfaction with the car and service. This feedback is crucial for improving service and sales approaches.

In Japan, customer service is taken even further, with almost every business greeting customers at the door. This practice exemplifies exceptional business conduct.

Moreover, receipts at restaurants and fast food chains often include a survey invitation, allowing customers to comment on the food quality, service, and even the cleanliness of the facilities. This method has been extended to hospitals, clothing stores, malls, and public bathrooms, sometimes employing instant survey devices to maintain high standards.

Corporations also conduct internal surveys to address employee concerns, asking direct questions about workplace treatment and management. This approach helps foster a workplace environment based on equality and respect for basic human rights.

U.S. colleges and universities also utilize feedback techniques to enhance their teaching methods and select the best professors. Toward the end of the academic year, administrations distribute written surveys to students, asking for their opinions on courses and instructors. This allows students to express their views on professor performance and course content. The collected data helps the administration make informed decisions about courses and faculty appointments. Colleges aim to retain top-quality professors to uphold their integrity, prestige, and educational standards. This approach also motivates professors to excel in their roles or risk termination.

It is in the best interest of any government to educate its citizens effectively. Governments should use commercials, publicity, outdoor billboards, and even propaganda to foster better citizenship. Educating people is often easier, cheaper, and faster than addressing problems after they arise, where the government must expend resources and effort to rectify issues. By proactively educating citizens, they become more invested in their country and work towards making it cleaner, stronger, and more advanced.

Spending and Distributing Free Money

Encouraging spending is beneficial for the economy. Governments should motivate citizens to spend money to sustain economic health. A well-managed economy is crucial for national survival, with the government playing a key role.

Industrial and Agricultural Expansion: Build sufficient factories, plants, farms, and offices to employ the working class.

Construction Projects: Initiate new construction projects or renovate existing structures to create jobs and maintain infrastructure.

Boost Production: Focus on extensive production to generate employment, provide affordable goods, and ensure consumers have access to inexpensive products.

Promote Competition: Encourage competition among companies to produce cost-effective, high-quality products. Attractive, reasonably priced goods will entice consumers to make purchases.

Marketing and Promotion: Enable companies to advertise their products through state and private media—radio, TV, newspapers, and magazines—to draw consumers to buy more.

Educational Campaigns: Inform the public about the benefits of spending and the economic goals behind consumer activity.

Consumer Participation: Engage consumers in the economic process. They play a critical role in the health of the economy and should take active responsibility for its growth. As John F. Kennedy famously encouraged, "Ask not what your country can do for you—ask what you can do for your country." Robust consumer spending drives high production and supply, making goods and services more affordable and available, thus sustaining employment and economic stability.

Consumers' active involvement in spending helps safeguard jobs and promotes a robust economic cycle.

It is vital for developing countries with abundant resources to share the wealth with their citizens. The revenue from these resources should be distributed to the citizens in the form of cash or checks, either mailed or deposited directly. This step is crucial for the economic well-being of the nation. These checks should be spent within a specified period. Countries like Norway, Saudi Arabia, and Kuwait already share revenue from national resources with their citizens in various forms.

As previously mentioned, to keep the economic cycle steady and directed properly, citizens need extra money to spend on both needs and wants. When citizens have disposable income, they tend to purchase additional goods and services, necessitating increased production from companies to meet this demand. The more consumers buy, the more factories need to produce, and the more workers are retained. Suppose a government sends checks to 10 million families across the country. Each family will likely need to buy something—many will purchase new cars, renovate their homes, buy new furniture, TVs, refrigerators, computers, cell phones, clothes, go on vacation, or simply buy food. The intention is for this money to be spent quickly, not saved, as hoarding cash in banks or safes does not stimulate the economy. Therefore, the money must be spent within a certain time frame until the next check is issued. When consumers make these purchases, they drive factories, plants, and farms to increase the production of these items.

It is in the country's self-interest to have local or national factories, plants, and shops to produce various items such as goods, tools, machines, gadgets, and cars. Otherwise, it will lead to zero economic activity. Purchasing imported goods and services will annihilate the economy of that particular country because local consumers will incentivize foreign companies, factories, and plants to produce more instead of local and national companies.

Immigrants

Immigrants can significantly contribute to the economy of their homeland. They can participate effectively in improving the economy by investing in various sectors. If a country lacks the resources or funds to build factories and assembly lines, the government should facilitate market entry for immigrants and make it easy for them to access resources to provide goods and services for those remaining in the homeland. Immigrants can invest in housing, establish factories, or supply markets with essential tools and machines, involving themselves in every sector possible to alleviate the government's burden.

Immigrants, for instance, can significantly impact the automotive sector by sending cars to their homelands, where cars are much cheaper. Cars are a critical tool for creating millions of jobs. More cars on the streets means the government needs to build more roads and highways, covering thousands of miles. This construction will require thousands of workers, thereby creating numerous jobs.

The second step involves the need for gas stations due to the increased number of cars. Gas stations will require staff to operate them and truck drivers to deliver not only gas but also various items, especially if the stations include convenience stores. These stores might stock dairy items, toiletries, over-the-counter medicines, candy, snacks, automotive supplies, hot food, batteries, and water, among others.

The third step necessitates the construction of these gas stations, which are equipped with computers, fridges, coffee makers, and soda machines and often offer pizzas and sandwiches. Consider how many people are involved in operating just one gas station. To satisfy the needs of American drivers, there are over 145,000 gas stations, averaging almost 3,000 stations per state—a substantial number that employs nearly 1 million people, not including the workers in factories that produce items for these gas stations.

Step four, if the gas station doubles as a convenience store, it would encourage factories to produce more. According to the Illinois Department of Commerce, a small convenience store should stock an average of 300 items. By selling all these items, hundreds of factories will participate in making this gas station function effectively. These hundreds of factories will obviously need thousands of employees.

Step five: if a country has millions of cars, imagine how many dealers, mechanics, and car washes are needed to sell, fix, and maintain these cars—thousands, isn't it? In addition, each store can specialize in fixing certain aspects of those cars; for instance, some may specialize in welding, others in mechanical repairs, some in oil services, some in changing tires only, others in painting, and some in changing batteries and brakes.

Step six, if a government allows the circulation of millions of cars, the owners have to buy registration, inspection, and insurance from the government. The government would generate millions of dollars which can be used for various purposes. Additionally, to manage all this—registration, inspection, and insurance—we would need thousands more employees.

Driving licenses are another way of generating revenue and creating more jobs for young people. I am going to be a little cynical by saying, "More cars means more accidents, which is good for the economy." Some economists think that disasters, floods, hurricanes, earthquakes, accidents, and even death are good for the economy. If millions of cars are running in a country, the likelihood of accidents increases. Car accidents mean more paramedics will be needed, more cars to be repaired, more cars to be sold, more car parts to be sold, more doctors to be visited, more medicine to be purchased, more money charged by insurance companies, and the list goes on. Everyone will be busy, and all of this can be facilitated by hiring more and more employees.

Step eight, more cars, means more speeding tickets, which in turn means that the government would generate millions of dollars. According to the Speeding Tickets Facts website in the US, for instance, over six billion dollars in revenue is generated annually through speeding tickets. So, imagine how much money governments in developing countries can collect every year from the vast number of cars circulating on their roads. Moreover, to issue these tickets and collect all this money, we need to hire many police officers and clerks.

Having millions of cars in a country means we need hundreds of stores that sell car parts. However, it would be fascinating and beneficial if that country were manufacturing all those parts. Millions of jobs can be created since each car contains an average of 30,000 parts, from the tiniest nuts and bolts to the engine block.

Having millions of cars also means that roads require maintenance. It also necessitates more traffic lights and their production. Additionally, millions of cars mean thousands of traffic signs are needed, and their maintenance is required.

More lights and posts and their maintenance are needed on highways, bridges, boulevards, and streets. So, in a perfect society, a family would need at least two cars to run its errands. Let's say a country has 10 million families; then 20 million cars are needed for this society to make their life easy and pleasant. With 20 million cars running on the roads, we can faithfully create millions of jobs.

In conclusion, governments in developing countries need to step up and allow immigrants to send money or remittances to take part in building the economies of their countries and help their compatriots to be happy. Remittances can raise domestic consumption of goods and services, and reduce poverty. Remittances give countries the opportunity to fund new projects and hire more people. In 2022, remittances to India, for example, were at $100 billion, and to Mexico were estimated at $60 billion; this provides an important source of much-needed funds. Compatriots, on their end, need to step in and take part in making all of this achievable. Returning migrants, with their higher tendency and experience, can develop their businesses at home; they have seen how businesses are run in developed countries and can apply those techniques and ways of doing things at home.

Banking and Trust

For an economy to remain stable or reach high peaks, citizens also have to trust the local banks. To achieve this, the government must promise to protect the money saved in banks in case of loss, theft, or any unfortunate bank dealings or investments. By doing so, citizens will have confidence in the government, be at peace, and finally deposit more money in those banks. The Federal Deposit Insurance Corporation (FDIC) in the US, for instance, was established to restore trust in the American banking system. This agency can cover up to $250,000 in insurance per depositor, a smart way to maintain stability and public confidence in the nation's financial system.

All local banks need people's savings to function and survive; they use that money for multiple investments and projects to generate more income. When banks perform very well, they can make millions of dollars and will eventually adapt to any economic crisis that might distress the economy. The government also needs that money to pay all federal employees and to ensure all federal offices function properly. However, it must return depositors' money whenever they need it to build unconditional trust.

Banks must also introduce new technologies like credit cards and online banking. Credit cards mean less cash in circulation and fewer notes being printed. Printing more cash often leads to inflation, which is hard to recover from. Moreover, printing money itself costs money. For example, printing a one-dollar bill in the US costs 5.4 cents, while printing a $100 bill costs 15 cents. Shockingly, according to DW news, after decades of independence, about two-thirds of the 54 African countries still import their currencies from France, Germany, the UK, or North America. They do so for security reasons and because they claim it is cheaper.

Ironically, in 2018, Ghana, for instance, paid about $92,000 just in shipping fees. The printing companies charge countries based on the requirements for designs, security features on each note, and the number of denominations to be made.

Printing currencies overseas sometimes results in a shortage of liquid money, raising questions about real autonomy, national security, and national pride.

If a country decides to print new currency, this latter should look really nice and be meaningful to maintain its value and condition. For banknotes to remain safe, clean, and last for a long time, they should be made from synthetic polymer.

Countries such as Australia, the UK, Canada, Vietnam, Mexico, and Morocco have introduced polymer notes. These notes are waterproof, dirt-proof, have a long lifespan, are hard to counterfeit, and are easy to recycle. Money should carry names and pictures of significant leaders who influenced the nation's history, and why not of world-famous scientists who influenced people's lives, so new generations can be inspired to be good citizens and good leaders.

Banks are supposed to aggressively motivate businessmen to borrow money to help with the economy. They should allow businesspeople to borrow as much money as they want with the primary purpose of boosting the economy and creating jobs. They could also make a list of all the sectors that need improvement in the country as the first condition for lending money. The second condition is to hire people. This is a smart way to supply the country with all types of goods and services and also a very effective way to create thousands of jobs.

Multiple Holidays Are Good for the Economy

Multiple holidays are a good way to keep the economy running to a certain degree. To explain this, I will use the US as an example, as it has more holidays than any other country in the world. There is roughly one holiday per month in the US, and each holiday is celebrated to the fullest. As a result, companies, supermarkets, clothing, and jewelry stores benefit greatly from these holidays by selling their products continuously. For instance, New Year's Eve is a holiday where almost all restaurants are booked for celebrations. Consequently, restaurants order tons of meats, poultry, pasta, vegetables, sauces, cakes, and drinks. In preparation for this day, farmers produce more fruits, vegetables, eggs, and an abundance of meat and poultry. Bakeries stock up on wheat and flour prior to this holiday to make a variety of cakes to sell to restaurants. Drink manufacturers also get busy during this holiday trying to meet the demand from all venues celebrating this global event.

Obviously, these companies, bakeries, restaurants, and farms would need additional help—workers, drivers, servers, cooks. At the time of this holiday, more people are hired than in any other season. This episode leads to the creation of seasonal jobs, and surprisingly, these seasonal jobs sometimes become permanent.

In preparation for the second holiday, which falls on February 14th—Valentine's Day—farmers plant and sell more flowers, jewelry stores sell more gold and diamonds, and restaurants and clothing stores are extremely busy. During this celebration, many businesses are busy designing, making, producing, transporting, and selling their products. Each item requires hundreds, if not thousands, of people to produce and stay busy until the next holiday.

In May, there are two major holidays: Mother's Day and Memorial Day. During Mother's Day, restaurants and clothing stores are extremely busy, which means clothing factories must produce more, and restaurants need to plan extensively to accommodate the large number of guests celebrating this respected holiday. At the end of May comes Memorial Day, a day when Americans honor and mourn the US military personnel who have died while serving in the armed forces. It is a paid holiday, and many people travel to visit family members in different parts of the US. It is a significant celebration, and people spend a lot of money either by going out to places, restaurants, or the shore. Either way, companies continue producing, and workers maintain their employment.

The biggest holiday in the US is Christmas. Christmas is the largest economic stimulus for many countries around the globe, significantly increasing production and sales in nearly all retail sectors during this popular holiday. Supply and demand for both goods and services surge around Christmas. In 2022, it was estimated that $876 billion was spent on Christmas gifts and retail sales. Such an amount compels every facet of any company to boost production, distribution, and sales of its products.

Thanksgiving is another major holiday in the US, with millions of people traveling to celebrate with their families. According to American data, Thanksgiving is the busiest air travel day in the US. Additionally, grocery stores experience soaring sales of consumer products ranging from red and white meats to various kinds of drinks and candy. In 2020, sales for Thanksgiving surpassed $5 billion.

In addition to Halloween and Labor Day, there's Father's Day... not to mention regular birthdays that almost every single person celebrates. While some people spend modestly on birthdays, others spend lavishly; however, if you consider that the US has 320 million residents celebrating their birthdays, there would be over 800,000 birthdays a day. Imagine the amount spent on clothes, jewelry, cakes, drinks, flowers, and the cost of throwing parties for these occasions. Developing countries ought to recognize that holidays and celebrations are beneficial for the economy. Each holiday provides numerous businesses the opportunity to earn money and sustain their employees.

Schools should also have opportunities to generate funds to cover at least some of their expenses. Sometimes, school districts don't have enough money to offer free lunch for kids. In some developing countries, schools lack basic amenities like windows, adequate tables, school supplies, heating, or water. Therefore, they should be allowed to use their classrooms, gyms, amphitheaters, and cafeterias for hosting events such as conventions, meetings, conferences, and celebrations like engagements, weddings, baby showers, and birthdays—especially during summer holidays.

Conclusion

Although developing countries possess the resources and necessary means to launch an economy, they often fail to do so. Many known and unknown causes remain stumbling blocks. Some causes are political, others are economic, and some remain enigmatic. This book addresses these problems and outlines how to establish an economic infrastructure that can lead to a strong future economy.

It is not only the responsibility of governments to lead the way but also of the citizens. They are the ultimate decision-makers in their country. Both governments and citizens in developing countries must bear in mind that there is no more time to waste. They should embark on implementing these steps to move their countries forward. They must also remember that no one will come to their rescue; we live in a harsh world where survival is for the strongest.

This book provides an overview of how to initiate a new era of economic development for a struggling economy in a specific country at a particular time. For more information and details on how to implement these steps, you can email me at mattbsellama@gmail.com. I will be more than happy to help.

www.ingramcontent.com/pod-product-compliance
Lightning Source LLC
Chambersburg PA
CBHW052117030426
42335CB00025B/3027